# The Gathering Table

## Defying MS With a Year of Pasta, Wine & Friends

Ronda Giangreco

With a foreword
by renowned chef,
Michael Chiarello

This book is dedicated to my father-in-law, Corrado
Giangreco who, through his courageous example,
showed his son how to be a steadfast, loyal
and loving partner in the face of Multiple Sclerosis

# Foreword

**C**ooking truly is one of life's greatest meditations, even more so when you serve your food to the people you care about most. As a young boy, my culinary mentor, best friend, and mother taught me that whatever is going on outside the kitchen simply doesn't touch you once you are within. My father was disabled and I watched firsthand as my mother would gladly retreat to the kitchen to find peace from worry while preparing our family's meals for the day. Inviting me in was always a great treat. She told me stories about her family, of both graces and hardships, while I sat across the table from her peeling garlic. Even when I watched her alone in the kitchen it brought me great joy to see happiness emanate from her as she prepared the dishes to be brought to our table. Twenty years later and the gift she gave me as a boy, I, in turn, was obligated to give back. Restaurant after restaurant, book after book, TV show after TV show all with the same purpose: to share with those who cared the amazing gift it is to prepare food in order to serve others.

Enter Ronda with the crushing news of a debilitating medical diagnosis and her wondrous story of perseverance in the face of pain. She met her hardship with a plan in her hand and courage in her heart. I remember dearly our first meeting and how small I felt compared to the mountain ahead of her. I was touched that I could be even the slightest help in her move towards the weekly serving of others. Our Eastern-minded friends believe that servitude is the evolution of one's spirit preparing for transformation and Ronda was clearly ready for that journey. Going home that evening, I was humbled by our encounter and hopeful she would find the joy and healing I had been taught to find, and continue to find, in the kitchen and in serving others.

Roll forward more than two years later, and in comes Ronda for lunch over the 2011 holiday season. Book in hand and a great tale to tell. As I sat with her, tears welled up in our eyes, no words needed to be spoken. Her presence at Bottega for lunch that day was a symbol of her strength. Here she was, still on her feet, long after her doctors leveled their diagnosis that she only had twelve good months left. Once again I found myself humbled in her presence.

I am of firm belief that reading her book will inspire you to create a lifelong series of flavor memories shared with those you love. And there really is a gigantic difference between taste and flavor. Taste only occurs in one's mouth. Flavor is gathered through hours spent in the kitchen and at the table surrounded by loved ones with stories being told.

Take this book and learn from the gifts she is sharing. Commit one or fifty-two days with those you love and start your legacy now.

*Michael Chiarello*

*January 2012*
*Chef/Owner, Bottega Ristorante in Yountville, CA*
*Author of **Bottega: Bold Italian Flavors from the Heart of California's Wine Country***

*Fate* is like a strange, unpopular restaurant, filled with odd waiters who bring you things you never asked for and don't always like.

**~Lemony Snicket**

## one

"I had an epiphany last night, Michael."

"Not another one," he mumbled, heaving a theatrical sigh.

"Just listen. I've decided I'm going to host a dinner party every Sunday for a year, starting on the first Sunday in January. I'll invite a bunch of friends, your brother and Anita, and our boys. And I'll make a big Italian feast like your Grandma Giangreco used to do."

"How the hell are you going to do that?" my husband muttered while staring intently at the sports page.

Twice I had been to cooking school in Italy. If I could manage to stay on my feet, and not give in to the crushing fatigue that often plagued me, I might be able to pull it off.

"You always say the only thing you can control is your attitude. If I just stay positive and think of myself as healthy, I know I could do it."

Peering over the rim of my coffee cup I waited to see if he would challenge his favorite line of advice. In the chess match that is marriage, familiarity is your most effective weapon. Although his eyes never left the newspaper, I noticed that his pupils were no longer moving. He was searching for a good counter argument.

"You're going to visualize yourself healthy enough to cook a big dinner every Sunday for a year?"

"Yeah, why not?"

*"For fifty-two weeks in a row?"*

It was an audacious proposition but it beat the hell out of shopping for wheelchairs. I had been slumped on the couch all morning listing the things I might soon be unable to do, a miserable way to start my day. I was facing a life that was about to disintegrate into a pathetically tragic tale, so even an irrational plan was an appealing alternative. I'd make a run for my favorite room in the house while I was still on my feet. My snug, dependable kitchen, the one place where I always found solace and a sense of purpose seemed like the perfect port in which to take cover from the gathering storm. The plan was a damned sight better than just sitting around in stomach-churning anticipation of my next medical crisis and it provided an answer to the question that had been plaguing me for the past several weeks.

*If I wasn't going to be walking for much longer, where should I walk now?*

Finding the right answer was suddenly a fundamental and urgent requirement. Until recently, I had blithely disregarded the possibility of any barrier to my enjoyment of a full and rich life.

Back in my early thirties, I had made a list of one hundred things I wanted to do, see, taste and feel. I recorded such wildly dissimilar and ambitious goals as meeting the Dali Lama and placing a scandalously large bet in Monte Carlo. I had vowed that someday I would sew a quilt and catch a really big fish. I wanted to swim naked in the ocean, dance the Tango in a Spanish bar and witness the grandeur of the Aurora Borealis. I envisioned myself testifying before Congress and even saving someone's life. The one-hundredth entry? Live, *really live*, until I was ready to die. Now that the inescapable finale was staring me down, I realized my final entry might prove most challenging of all.

"How about if I just start with this Sunday and see what happens from there? I'll make your favorite pistachio gelato for dessert."

He looked up from the newspaper and grinned widely. Checkmate.

Of course I had no intention of cooking only one dinner. In fact, the more I thought about it, the more elaborate the scheme became. I'd create an e-mail list of everyone I knew and send out invitations each week. The first six who accepted would make the guest list. And I'd write a blog about the dinners detailing the menus and conversations. And photos! I'd take scores of photos and put them in a nice album. I'd create a remembrance of what would probably be my last good year. I knew the odds were against me actually cooking for an entire year, but at least I would have some fun for a little while.

I would stay me.

*I look like the same person I have always been. I still believe the same things, think the same way, and behave in the same manner. In fact, in nearly every way you could describe a person, I'm identical to who I was six weeks ago. There are no missing limbs, no terrible wounds, but I am now damaged in a very fundamental way.*

*My immune system has decided to attack my spinal column, in stark contrast to what is in the best interests of the rest of my body. In a mere twenty-four hours, I have become a disabled woman. I am numb from the collarbone down, as though shot through with a bazooka of Novocain. My sense of touch sends wild signals to my brain. What was once soft, the belly fur of my dog, now feels like a scouring pad. Running my fingers through my own hair, I encounter a mass of fishing wire, coarse and artificial. I search for familiar clues to anchor me in the world. Awkward and unbalanced, I find they don't exist anymore.*

*This state of affairs is oddly fascinating as well as frightening. It is also impossible to believe it is not temporary, that I won't wake up tomorrow and have my old body, my old life returned to me.*

In looking back at how it all began, the most startling aspect of the day my life changed forever was how innocuously the portents of misfortune presented themselves. On a summer morning, Michael and I were preparing to drive from our home in Auburn, California, to the Napa Valley for an afternoon of wine tasting. While brushing my teeth I noticed an odd sensation just under my chin. The area was curiously tingling. Even though there was no redness or swelling, I assumed the minor irritation was due to an insect bite of some sort. Throughout the day, I kept putting my hand to my neck as the sensitivity of the area became increasingly bothersome—though certainly not ominous.

Our friends had rented a limousine for a tour of several wineries. Afterward, we stopped by a gourmet market and picked up the fixings for a grand feast to enjoy on their deck which featured a panoramic view of the wine country. From our lofty perch we watched red-tailed hawks soaring and diving over vineyards that stretched high up the flanks of the grassy, rolling hills surrounding the Napa Valley. As it set, the sun saturated the vines with a tawny glow, making them appear gilded, even gaudy. The exaggerated display was an appropriate ending to our afternoon of excess.

At one point in the evening our host went down into his wine cellar and came back with an expensive, older vintage cabernet he had been saving for a special occasion, announcing that just such a night warranted its uncorking. We toasted our good fortunes and wondered aloud what we had done to deserve such a life. As the evening wound down Michael and I made our way to the guest room and remarked that we would remember this day forever. The next morning I awoke to discover that almost the entire left side of my body was numb. My first thought was that I had perhaps enjoyed a bit too much wine during the evening and slept on that side all night without moving.

"Just shake your leg and rub your arm," Michael instructed me.

But even after hobbling awkwardly around the room and massaging my left arm, no sensation returned to my limbs. When nothing had changed after an hour, Michael, as well as our friends, began to worry. They all insisted I call the hospital. When I reached a nurse and explained my symptoms she instructed me to chew three aspirins and call an ambulance. She felt certain that I'd had a stroke. Not wanting to ramp up the drama around what I was sure was a much less serious problem, I had Michael drive me to the emergency room.

With a parade of nurses coming and going, technicians drawing blood, and doctors ordering tests, we were no closer to an explanation for the strange symptoms.

Holding Michael's hand tightly, I told him, "I have a sinking feeling I've just taken the first step toward a place I'm not going to like."

"No way. You'll be fine. I'm sure any minute now the doctor will come in and give us a reasonable explanation for all of this," he assured me.

With minutes stretching into hours, we waited for test results. Ultimately, I was indeed diagnosed with a stroke and admitted to the hospital...but I knew I could not have had a stroke. I've always had low blood pressure, and the numbness did not encompass my entire side; the pieces just didn't fit. Yet there was one point on which the doctors and I could certainly agree—something was very wrong with my body.

When I awoke the next morning in the hospital, I discovered that my right side was numb as well. The diagnosis of stroke was promptly discarded, and our belief in a simple rationale for all this craziness faded. The doctors tested for HIV, lupus, Lyme's disease, and other equally unsettling possibilities. Had I recently traveled outside the country? Had I noticed any other unusual warning signs? Even CT scans, multiple blood tests, and examinations by a wide range of specialists produced no clear answers as to what was causing my increasingly bizarre array of symptoms. But four days later, after two MRIs and a painful spinal tap, the doctors finally concluded I had idiopathic Transverse Myelitis, a rare neurological disease with a poor prognosis for recovery. This happened, they told me, because my immune system had turned on me, eating away at the myelin sheath that protected my nerves. The damage was causing my nervous system to send inaccurate messages to my brain. They had found a lesion on my spinal column at T2, high up at the base of my neck. "Transverse" meant that it spanned the width of my spine. "Myelitis" referred to the inflammation the lesion was causing and "idiopathic" meant they didn't know why the hell it had happened. What surprised them most was that I still had control of my bowels and bladder, the loss of which is a common symptom of the disorder. I credited my heightened sense of dignity for the lucky break I had received.

With some hint of hope, I hung onto the fact that a small percentage of people regained a measure of their mobility and sensation over time, but after six months whatever improvement I might experience would be all that was coming. They prescribed steroids to reduce the inflammation and gave me sedatives to help offset the side effect of sleeplessness the drug caused. Otherwise, that was all the medical community had to offer me.

On the plus side, I was getting a lot of wonderful attention. My sons, Daniel and Patrick, had come rushing to my side at the hospital. The shock on their faces and tears in their eyes as they stood at the foot of my bed were both painful and touching to witness. They had never seen their hard-charging mother in such a fragile state. Both inherited my optimistic attitude, though, and when a physical therapist suggested that a certain very popular and difficult-to-obtain game system might help me regain my balance, they were off and running. On a mission, they searched, begged and schemed to buy one for me. Finally, a kindhearted store clerk believed the story about their neurologically damaged mother and set a game system aside for them. They were positive they had secured the means of fixing this mess.

Dozens of friends also stopped by to boost my spirits and brought so many floral arrangements that my hospital room was beginning to resemble a parade float.

Michael doled out just the right amount of concern over the situation, along with confidence about my recovery. He left the hospital to go home and prepare our house in Auburn for my return, laying in the supplies, drugs and devices that would enable me to stay out of a rehabilitation ward. He purchased a chair and handheld nozzle for the shower, installed handrails, rearranged the furniture to accommodate my various pieces of medical equipment, and set up the "miracle cure" computerized game system.

After a week I was discharged from the hospital with a walker, a body I could no longer feel and hands that shook and refused to obey my commands. In an effort to scratch my nose I'd end up poking myself in the eye. My sense of touch was wildly out of whack, as well. The skin on my legs and feet felt almost reptilian, scaly and coarse, although Michael kept assuring me they were as soft and smooth as they had always been. And in a weird, almost comical way, my feet felt like they were encased in bubble wrap. Walking is a real challenge when you're not able to feel your feet touching the floor. I also developed this eerie sensation called L'Hermitte's Syndrome. The act of bending my neck and looking down would cause a bizarre electric charge to race up my spine. It wasn't painful, just peculiar. It was amazing how many times I got "shocked" before I learned to not look down. Lab rats are undoubtedly quicker on the uptake.

While these changes were deeply disturbing, I was in no pain. In fact, if I could have been assured that everything would return to normal in a few days, I might have even found my circumstances rather entertaining in a horrifying sort of way. I wasn't dying. There were no scars or broken limbs. And really, other than the emotional distress this was causing, I was in no discomfort. I had always been healthy, kept my weight in check, had regular check-ups and exercised. So nothing really bad could happen to me, right? I was sure this was all some sort of cosmic error and I'd be myself again soon.

The doctors weren't blaming my predicament on any activity, genetics or lack of vigilance over my well-being, though. It was exasperating that they weren't able to point to any identifiable cause for my sudden state of disability. I was not the only one frustrated by this ambiguity, either. My friends and family also wanted to know what had triggered this so they could avoid making the same mistake. There had to be a reasonable explanation, a cautionary tale to be learned from this. None of us likes to believe we are completely helpless against the capricious nature of fate. But with no reassuring clarification forthcoming, we all had to accept it might simply be my turn to receive the short straw.

Fortunately during the next couple of weeks, however, I showed signs of improvement. My hands became more controllable. I graduated from the dreaded walker to a fashionable cane, and my beloved standard poodle, Bella, was starting to feel like the warm, fluffy creature she had always been. Confident I would be among the minority who nearly completely regained their health, I had begun to look at this event as a mere footnote in my life. My incredible talent for good luck was holding.

Then, very early one morning, a new and terrifying symptom presented itself. I awoke from a sound sleep with a strange, twitchy feeling. Adrenalin pumping through my veins, I experienced an overwhelming "fight or flight" sensation. Suddenly my body became wracked with violent tremors, my legs and arms shaking uncontrollably. Michael bolted up and wrapped his arms around me while reaching for the phone to call an ambulance. I kept insisting he shouldn't. Whatever was happening, it would surely stop soon. An ambulance would make it all too real.

So he held me in the dark, and we waited.

After agonizingly long minutes the tremors eventually subsided. I vowed to call my neurologist as soon as his office opened and we both tried to banish the shock of what had just happened. When I reached my doctor he was adamant that if another episode of tremors occurred we should call an ambulance immediately. Only a couple of days later my body once again went into a state of furious disorder. This time Michael didn't hesitate to summon for help.

"I'm fairly certain you have Devic's Disease," the doctor announced and then promptly hurried out of my hospital room, providing few details about this new and frightening turn of events. The nurses were unfamiliar with the rare diagnosis and could offer little in the way of information. Finally, a kind, elderly volunteer went downstairs and used an office computer to access the Internet and provide me with some facts about the disease. When she arrived back at my room with a handful of papers, she had tears in her eyes. She simply said, "I'm sorry sweetie," gave me a hug and left.

Those papers stayed face-down on my hospital bed while I tried to muster up the courage to read them. When I finally did the reality of what was in store for me hit in a tidal wave of fear, disbelief, and panic. Devic's Disease was a death sentence, and the path to the end would be a ghastly one that would likely include full paralysis and a complete loss of sight. There was no cure, no treatment, and no hope. I would die encased in a blind, immobile body.

I slammed shut the door to my room and crawled into my hospital bed. Curled in a fetal position, I waited for Michael to come help me make sense of the horrifying future I had been handed. All during that long, lonely morning, I circulated through a range of emotion, alternating between tears, terror, and seething anger. I was furious enough to charge headlong into battle, but how could I combat an enemy that dwelled within? I wanted to scream, to lash out at someone, but there was no one to hold responsible for this terrible affront.

After I was released from the hospital, Michael and I fled to the place where we were married, our beloved Avila Beach, near San Luis Obispo, California. On a quiet stretch of sand looking out over the Pacific, Michael and I held one another and tried to comprehend the unthinkable. Through the tears, I begged him to promise he would help me exit this world with dignity when I became incapacitated. And he did. No more heartbreaking a vow could be given.

I planned my funeral that day, instructing him to select a single stone from the beach and have it engraved with my name, the date of my birth, and the date of my death, followed by the title of my favorite song by John Lennon, "Imagine." He was to then return with the rock and my ashes. I wanted him to place both on the sand and allow the waves to wash them out to sea.

As terrified as I was, I knew I would not be alone in this journey. Michael would be right at my side. But I also realized that he, too, would suffer greatly as this disease progressed. When he left the hotel room to get us something to eat, I used my walker to navigate the path to the edge of the cliffs overlooking the ocean. If I truly loved him, shouldn't I spare him the pain of watching me deteriorate? If there was indeed no hope, why prolong the agony? Jumping seemed like the most compassionate and rational act I could commit.

Frozen with fear, I grasped the railing and looked down at the dark ocean churning furiously below me. Would I regret my decision moments after releasing my grip? Would death come quick or would I suffer for hours in cold, hostile waters? A bleak fog crept up the sides of the sheer cliffs, increasing the despondency that was propelling me to a decision. The voice of optimism that had always bolstered me through the roughest patches of my life was strangely quiet.

But as I began to imagine the bewilderment Michael would experience at finding the room empty and silent, I hesitated. He'd be puzzled by the sight of the abandoned walker next to the railing. I could picture him calling for me, certain I was nearby. With growing apprehension he'd walk slowly toward the cliffs, his gaze falling to the jagged rocks below. The surging waves ebbing and eddying around my torn and broken limbs would provide a heartbreaking and unshakable final image. Worse yet, I knew he would blame himself. He had left me alone. Not my slow decline, but my dreadful, lonely death would surely prove to be the heavier burden. I could not hang that millstone around his neck.

I shuddered at the thought that I had even considered committing suicide when two weeks later the doctor called to inform me that he had, in fact, been wrong. A simple blood test proved I didn't have Devic's Disease after all. What the tests now conclusively pointed to was late onset Multiple Sclerosis. The irritating sensation that caused only a passing concern two months earlier had actually been the opening salvo in the attack the disease was now mounting against my spinal cord, brain, and optic nerves.

I immediately found another neurologist and began to come to terms with this new reality. Yes, Multiple Sclerosis is a terrible disease, but researchers seemed to be closing in on some promising treatments and it was a damned sight better than the previous diagnosis. But this particular disease packed a potent punch for us.

When Michael was a small child, his mother had been diagnosed with a particularly dreadful version of this same disease. Primary Progressive MS is the most aggressive form of Multiple Sclerosis, with no periods of remission, just a steady loss of mobility, sensation, and quality of life. She succumbed to complications of the disease at age forty-six. MS entered Michael's life when he was just a boy, and took his mother from him when he was a teenager. Thirty-five years later it had come back for his wife. The appalling improbability of such a cruel twist of fate was not lost on either of us.

Early in our relationship, Michael told me about his mother's heartbreaking and abbreviated life. Following a brief explanation, however, he rarely mentioned her. His standard response to my inquiries was simply, "My mother was sick and then she died." I thought the subject was too painful for him to discuss, but over time I began to realize that her illness had so come to define her that her own son actually knew very little about the "real" Mary Giangreco. She had been reduced in many ways from a whole and unique person to simply a tragedy. Furthermore, one day as I was dusting the only photograph we had of her Michael's youngest son, Tony, asked me, "Who is the lady in the picture?" Her grandson did not know who she was.

I decided then and there that I would honor her by writing her life story. Without Michael's knowledge, I contacted dozens of relatives, old friends and neighbors. All had poignant stories to tell of this compassionate and loving woman. Each day when Michael left for his office, I set her photograph next to my computer and went to work reconstructing her life for those she left behind. Along with a lengthy and tender letter from Michael's father, I also had copious notes from my long-distance phone conversations with her now elderly friends. They sent dozens of photographs of Mary in her youth, standing strong and healthy, smiling in that same mischievous manner she would someday pass on to her sons. When I finally finished my project, I had a dozen copies of the little book printed out and bound for my husband, his two sons, his brother, their father and members of Mary's family. And I gave a copy to Mary's mother on her one-hundredth birthday.

While writing the book, I began to feel a certain kinship with this woman, the mother-in-law whom I was never to meet. Through the memories of others, I had found a woman of humor and grace, someone whom I undoubtedly would have enjoyed knowing. I think she would have liked me, too. There was much we had in common. Yet I never would have guessed that the similarities between us would one day include the diagnosis of MS.

On the morning when I returned from my first hospitalization, I found that Michael had prepared the house for my arrival with flowers on the tables and my favorite foods in the refrigerator. After setting up all the things I would need to make my life easier, in what he considered to be a supreme act of thoughtfulness, he added one special touch for my homecoming. And it almost took me to my knees.

He had tenderly placed the framed photo of his mother on my pillow. He told me he had pleaded with her every night, begging her to intercede in some fashion, to do what she could to save me from her fate.

That photograph was a staggering reminder of what was in store for me. I didn't even want to look at it. I wanted to run from that room, but all I could manage to do was to stand, clutching my walker, and weep. He thought I was deeply touched by his kindhearted and loving gesture. I never had the heart to tell him how horrified I was at the sight of that photograph on my pillow.

I knew all of this was painful for him, too, and he was doing his best to deal with this dreadful twist of fate. Poor guy. He had allowed himself to love and be loved again, not knowing MS was waiting to deliver yet one more devastating blow. What were the odds that a fifty-three-year old, perfectly healthy woman would contract the same disease that had killed his mother? Worst of all, behind the concern I saw a hint of irrational guilt in his eyes. I knew he was thinking that this terrible disease had entered our lives through him.

In his early thirties, Michael had experienced a few episodes of optic neuritis, an early sign of impending MS. Fortunately he never developed full blown MS. But it had plans for him anyway. He just never imagined it would be me who would be struck down. He was supposed to be the prey.

So we danced to a new tune, two victims of overwhelming odds. I wouldn't have blamed him if he had bolted for the door. But, of course, he stayed. We would face this challenge together.

Little had we known what life had in store for us when we met on that summer afternoon in 1995. Back then I was the co-owner of a monthly magazine in Napa, California, and he was the newly hired publisher of the town's daily newspaper. We were competitors in our tiny market, battling it out for one-hundred-dollar shoe store ads. We weren't supposed to associate with one another much less fall in love. But as we eyed each other suspiciously at the Chamber of Commerce mixer, sizing up the enemy at hand, some cosmic switch clicked on.

I was forty, newly separated and hungering for a romantic adventure. He had just breezed into town a few weeks earlier, a ridiculously handsome Sicilian who oozed charm and sophistication. Every unattached woman in our small community was suddenly on red alert. To throw my hat into that particular ring was to invite certain heartache, but with my characteristic lack of restraint, I whipped off the beret and slung it. Sure enough, he didn't fail to deliver the goods.

No mascara ever invented could have withstood the onslaught of tears produced by our tumultuous relationship. Our on-again, off-again love affair became a common topic of conversation around the water coolers at our respective offices. After yet another inglorious break-up, I announced to a friend that we had patched things up and become a couple again. She pointedly asked, "A couple of what?"

Fools in love? We were more like morons mired in a game of mental torture. He refused to make a commitment to me in spite of the fact that we clearly loved one another. Hurt and confused by his tendency to cut and run whenever the intimacy between us reached a level that made him uncomfortable, I would lash out with a tearful tirade. The repeated break-ups were always preceded by spectacular rows. One even involved me hurling a candlestick at his head. Finally, I decided that for the emotional and physical health of us both, I would leave for good. I sold my share of the magazine, packed my bags, and headed out of town. Of course, the addition of a few hundred miles between us did little to quell the passion neither of us could deny. After a full year of forced separation, he called me. The sound of his voice on the phone caused my knees to wobble.

"I went to a psychic yesterday," Michael announced.

"You did *what*?"

Michael is a pragmatic soul. The thought of him extending his hand to a turbaned stranger to learn his fate was a scene difficult to imagine.

"She told me the woman who brought me to her was not the one I am supposed to be with."

Whoever she was, she had certainly taken a creative approach to wooing him. I wondered who in the long line of contenders was now hoping to take my place.

"Silly girl. She should have explained her motives and tipped the fortune-teller generously beforehand."

"I'm being serious here."

"Serious about some hippie chick with a crystal ball?"

"She had Tarot cards."

"I've heard they are unquestionably more accurate."

"Just listen. She told me I was destined to be with a woman who drives me nuts."

"I assume you're referring to me. I'm not sure if I should be flattered or offended."

"And she also said we had been together in many previous lives."

"So even in death you've never been able to get rid of me?"

"Exactly. Like a bad penny."

"I don't understand. What do you want me to do with this information?"

"Marry me."

At that preposterous suggestion and with no more sense than a couple of eighteen-year-olds, we ran off to the beach two weeks later and actually did the deed. Of course, we were too embarrassed to tell anyone until months later. We were somehow hoping that by gently exposing people to the idea of us as a pair again they'd all recognize the wisdom of our decision. No such luck. There was universal opposition from our adult children, our siblings, our friends, even our dry cleaner. No one thought this was a good idea. We privately joked that eloping had been our only option. Had we allowed a preacher to perform a ceremony in which he asked if anyone knew why we two should not be joined, the line of objectors would have stretched out of the chapel and around the block.

However, as the years of marital bliss accumulated no one was more astonished at the success of our match than the two of us. With time the early indicators of incompatibility disappeared and soon neither of us could even remember why we had ever behaved so unreasonably. We had weathered our combative courtship, quieted the naysayers and settled into a life we expected would present little in the way of challenges.

That assumption would prove to be terribly naive.

As if all of the misfortune related to my health wasn't enough, the clouds of financial trouble were gathering as well. In the latter months of 2008, we stood helplessly by as our hard-earned retirement dollars disappeared with each downward tick of the stock market. Coupled with the fact that the value of our home was declining almost daily, it was a nauseating ride.

The economy was also having a devastating effect on Michael's career. As an executive in the newspaper industry, he and his colleagues had witnessed a steady decline in revenue due to the Internet. The weakening economy was dealing the fatal blow to many newspapers across the country. We had moved from Napa, California, to Nashville, Tennessee, and then back to Auburn, California, as new opportunities presented themselves. But as one of his fellow publishers put it, they were all "riding dinosaurs into the tar pits."

In spite of his hard work and dedication, the group of newspapers he had been hired to manage in Placer County was suffering as well. When he met with the company's owners in early 2009, he was not surprised to hear that they could no longer afford to keep him on as their regional manager. But after the trials of the previous five months, the blow was almost too overwhelming to absorb. Fortunately, he worked for a family-owned company that cared deeply about its employees. The owner of the company, his son, and the president of the firm all knew of the health ordeal we were enduring. They offered Michael a position running their wine country visitor publication in Sonoma, California. It meant selling our home for much less than we had paid for it, and taking a deep cut in salary, but at least he would still have a job, and just as importantly, we would have the health insurance we now desperately needed.

We grudgingly accepted a $200,000 loss from the sale of our home and moved into a tiny rental condo. We were broken, beaten down and shell-shocked. How did everything go so wrong so fast? We knew we still had much to be thankful for. He had a job, we had each other, and surrounded by rolling greens hills and acres of vineyards, we were living in one of the most picturesque places in the country. But still, for the rest of that year the realization of all we had lost caused us to take turns dissolving into despair.

We had reasons to be optimistic as well, though. My health seemed to be holding up. Medication was keeping the tremors under control and no new symptoms had presented themselves. Michael was discovering that he loved his work for the first time in years and we were meeting many new friends in our little community. Most importantly, with some scrimping and saving, we managed to pull together a down payment for a new home. And I found what I believed to be a perfect little house for us to begin anew.

The tiny, pristine cottage was surrounded on all sides by towering, two-story homes. Like gigantic, wooly mammoths forming a protective circle around a newborn calf, the neighborhood appeared to be shielding its smallest member from harm.

"Geez, Ronda, are you kidding me? It looks like a little girl's playhouse," Michael grumbled.

Precisely. When I was growing up we lived on a small ranch in Southern California. In a remote corner of the property, beneath an ancient and gnarled olive tree, there was a miniature version of the main house. There I escaped from the turmoil of my parent's fractious marriage and created a picture-perfect home for myself with tea cups and dolls who never argued with one another. Fifty years later, I required another such place of refuge.

"But, honey, look. You can see the vineyards from the front porch."

Michael and I had managed to land in a sweet, often overlooked corner of the Northern California wine country. The prim little town of Sonoma is sandwiched between two glamorous and showy sisters. With posh Marin to the west and the famous Napa Valley to the east, Sonoma seemed content with her lot in life as the slightly plain, but good-natured farm girl of the family. The agricultural spirit of the area is apparent on nearly every street in town. Pastures with placid cows nestle between housing tracts. Neighbors place the excess bounty from their gardens on card tables in front of their homes, a tin can provided for payment on the honor system. Just blocks from downtown, over on Second Street, is an old barn that houses a team of enormous Clydesdale horses. Often in the morning, their owner slips a harness over their massive heads and hitches them up to a buckboard for a slow procession around town. The heavy, rhythmic clopping of their hoofs on the pavement is a sound that seems to belong to another century.

On the outskirts of town, rimmed by rolling, grass-covered hills, vineyards spread like verdant blankets. Every winter the showy vines shed their leaves and the valley floor takes center stage with mustard flowers so vibrantly yellow that they seem painted rather than planted.

The main road leading into town, Broadway, points itself directly at Sonoma's only adornment.

The wholesome, down-to-earth beauty of the Sonoma Plaza has a quintessential American feel to it. With its distinction as the largest and most famous town plaza in the state of California, it is the pride of the community. Its stalwart, two-story stone City Hall presides over family picnics and farmers' markets. The planners chose to design the building democratically, all four sides being identical, so that none of the surrounding businesses would face a less impressive façade. Towering trees, swing sets, and a pond encompassed by leggy reeds form the bucolic grounds that beckon Sonoma's citizens to just sit for awhile. Watch the children play. Feed the ducks.

Despite its lack of airs, the town does have a small element of haughtiness about it. The dividing line that separates the upper class from the merely fortunate is Broadway. Sonoma's eastside has been designated the tonier section of town, although an outsider would be hard-pressed to distinguish between the homes there and ones a mere block away on the "poor" side of town.

Steps from a meandering, tree-lined bike path that follows the route of a languid stream, the cottage was located just a short block from Broadway, on the more humble west side of town. With its modest stature, the diminutive house hardly seemed worthy of the battle that was ensuing over it.

Arms crossed, Michael declared, "I don't want to buy a house. Especially one that looks like it was built for gnomes."

It had taken weeks just to convince my husband to look at the house that had become an obsession for me. Now he was refusing to even enter it.

"Trust me. You're going to be amazed at how spacious it looks once you get inside."

"Impossible. It can't be more than twelve feet from one end to the other."

"Oh, please. It's at least thirty feet."

"That's counting the garage. Our suitcases and the lawnmower will have roomier quarters than we do."

What he didn't realize was, that although the front of the house did appear shockingly small, the home actually stretched far towards the back of the lot and wrapped around behind the garage. In a mere 1,200 square feet it managed to provide a kitchen, living room, dining room, two bedrooms, and two full bathrooms. In short, it was all the space we would ever need. Or more accurately, all the room I wanted.

As a passionate cook, I have always considered the kitchen the most important room in the house. I don't buy houses; I buy kitchens that happen to come with living rooms, bathrooms and bedrooms attached to them. This house had the smallest kitchen I've ever seen that wasn't on a boat or in a recreational vehicle. But the resourcefulness! Everything sat within reach with a host of perfect little alcoves for all my tools and utensils. There was not a speck of wasted real estate. I could picture myself rolling out pasta dough on the gleaming granite countertops, simply reaching behind me for my soup pot on the industrial wire shelves that lined the back wall. The kitchen reminded me of just the sort in which Alice Waters or Thomas Keller might have cooked in their early days. This was not a showplace; this was a workstation.

I have always been enamored of small spaces. The economical use of every inch in an organized demonstration of efficiency thrills me. I love nooks and crannies. Fortunately, Michael and I are both the opposite of packrats, preferring the prudent habit of acquiring only items we truly need or want rather than surrounding ourselves with useless knick-knacks. We were perfectly suited for small-house living; he just didn't know it yet.

We had always owned large houses even though for the majority of our ten-year marriage, it had been only the two of us living in them. Our four sons, two from his previous marriage and two from mine, had returned home from time to time but never stayed long before heading out to their next adventure. They were all grown men now, two with wives.

I knew that if I could just coax him in the door I could impress him with the home's best feature. A virtual forest of towering, leafy trees ringed the little backyard creating a resplendent sanctuary that sat like a secret behind the house's unassuming exterior. A private oasis in miniature.

It was just what we needed to repair our wounded bodies and spirits.

After a lot of grousing and negotiating he relented and let me have my diminutive haven. Sure enough, after moving into the home we felt as though the ground under us had stabilized a bit.

But a visit to my new doctor in late December left us wondering whether we were being a bit too complacent. He warned that my mobility would probably be compromised severely before long. We needed to plan ways of remodeling our new home to accommodate a wheelchair. From talk of ramps and widened doorways, we turned to the necessity for changes in the kitchen. That's when my resolve nearly failed me. Cooking was my passion, my means of expressing my love for Michael, for my family, and for my friends. A future that might exclude me from my kitchen was incomprehensible.

It was time to create a better future for myself. My idea for a year of dinner parties seemed like the perfect way to combat my growing fears. I'd grab hold of hope and run with it.

Elaborate, multi-course meals do not intimidate me. I have always gotten a kick out of planning and executing big dinner parties. I usually opt to tackle a complicated, time-consuming recipe I've never made before. It's a little like flying without a net: thrilling, but a bit reckless. You can deliver a spectacular performance, or you can crash and burn in front of your traumatized guests. There is rarely a middle ground, but that's the fun of it.

Michael used to think I was crazy to go to such lengths with the menus. He just didn't get it. One day as he was headed out to play eighteen holes I suggested he visit the miniature golf course instead. He looked at me as though I'd lost my mind.

"Why would I do that?"

"Well, it would be much easier. You wouldn't have to walk so far, you don't have to use anything but your putter and it's cheaper. Besides it's the same thing. You're still hitting a golf ball, aren't you?"

"Hitting a ball into a clown's mouth is not playing golf."

"And roasting hot dogs is not cooking."

It would be a long time before he suggested I make something simple again.

However, if I was going to pull off this year of dinner parties I needed to consider playing the windmill course myself. Any thoughts of attempting a dazzling display of culinary skills were replaced with the realization that a mere twenty minutes of exertion now required half an hour of recuperation. If I was going to make it through fifty-two of these affairs, I needed to be realistic about my capabilities.

Grabbing my favorite cookbook, an autographed copy of *At Home With Michael Chiarello*, I searched for a dish worthy of an inaugural meal but one that didn't require hours of time on my feet. A recipe for slow-braised short ribs, Brasciole style, lured me in with the thought of Chinese-style cross-cut ribs, thinly shaved garlic, fennel seeds, capers and Italian parsley simmering together for hours in a rich marinara sauce. Creating a platter of flavorful, falling-off-the-bone meat shouldn't be all that difficult. All I had to do was visit my favorite butcher for some nice marbled ribs, brine them for a few hours with salt water, brown sugar, juniper berries, and bay leaves, and then allow my oven to do the heavy lifting.

A simple little salad, some gelato in the ice cream maker and I had it covered. I couldn't resist trying one new recipe, though. Having never made homemade ricotta before I thought my first dinner party might just be the night to give it a try.

One twirl on the trapeze couldn't be too perilous, right?

*January 3rd – my first dinner party!*

## Menu:

*Homemade ricotta*
baked with fresh herbs,
served with toasted baguettes

*Field greens*
with balsamic vinaigrette

*Slow braised*
*Short ribs*
over creamy polenta

*Pistachio gelato*

## Guest List:

Susan & Alan
Scott & Mary
Tiera & Tracy

The first of my fifty-two dinner parties was everything I hoped it would be. The guest list combined both long-time friends and new acquaintances. Making the ricotta from scratch was much easier than I had thought it would be. And it was a real hit when served as an appetizer with toasted baguette slices. The braised ribs were much more complex, however, but with the detailed instructions provided by Chef Chiarello, I was able to breeze through the recipe. Much of the prep time involved letting the ribs marinate in the brine, and then slowly roast in the oven for hours, providing a marvelous aroma for greeting my guests. I served the meat over creamy polenta, garnishing the plate with rosemary, parsley, and lemon zest. The artful presentation elicited a level of awe that made all of the effort worthwhile. A simple salad was followed by that homemade pistachio gelato I had promised Michael.

As we ate lively topical banter gave way harrowing stories brought on by Michael's question, "What was the most fearful day of your life?" The evening was topped off with a hilarious story from our friend Tracy about her worst day as a dog groomer, during which she flawlessly played the part of each character in the tale, including that of a cheerful, tail-wagging pug. She related how, just as she was putting the finishing touches on her grooming job, she noticed a bit of lint in the corner of the dog's eye. As she rubbed the little pug's bulging eyelid its eye popped right out of the socket and rolled across the floor, landing at the feet of its owner! We were howling as she reenacted both her horror and the blasé reaction of the owner, who had failed to mention the animal's glass eye.

With laughter and great friends our adventure had begun. I was hopeful, committed to completing the task, and excited about the possibilities. Of course, one would have to be a bit certifiable to even consider embarking on fifty-two dinner parties in a row, especially with the diagnosis of a neurological disease. But impetuous, even a bit outrageous, escapades were not a rarity in my life. After all, I had tried my hand as a stand-up comedienne, hosted a radio talk show, explored an underground river in New Zealand, won thousands of dollars on the television game show *Sale of The Century*, and traveled to Europe alone in my fifties. In fact, it was my trips to Italy to attend cooking school that fueled my optimism about this newest challenge.

Michael had given me the gift of a week at a cooking school in Italy the year before all the tribulations befell us. I chose to make the experience unforgettable, selecting a school located in the exclusive restaurant, Quattro Passi, on the Amalfi Coast in southern Italy. This wasn't going to be a few days of playing in the kitchen with some nice, Italian housewife. I would be cooking alongside Chef Liberato, one of the most renowned chefs in the entire country. My accommodations would be in a stunning villa perched on a cliff that overlooked the bay of Naples in one direction and the bay of Salerno in the other. This would be a week I would savor for the rest of my life.

Not wanting to drag along anyone who wasn't an acknowledged culinary junkie, I declared that I would make the journey alone. On second thought, the idea of climbing aboard a jet that would take me halfway around the world to a place where I knew no one, couldn't speak the language, and didn't know where the hell I was going, caused waves of nausea to wash over me. Pathetic as it sounds, I had managed to live over five decades without ever having traveled by myself. However, with dozens of my fellow post-menopausal girlfriends expressing awe and admiration at my act of midlife courage, the weight of peer pressure was bearing down on me. I couldn't wimp-out.

By the time I found myself sitting in the airport waiting to board that plane I was nearly catatonic with fear. Like a beast to the slaughter, though, I trudged down the aisle and obediently took my seat. After hours of flight, and a couple of cocktails, boredom combined with the gin to give my heart a more measured rhythm. By the time I arrived in Munich, Germany, for a two-day layover, an inexplicable dose of bravado had kicked in. I couldn't wait to grab my bags and head off in search of adventure. It had dawned on me that far from home I was as much a stranger to everyone as they were to me. That realization was quickly followed by a scandalizing notion: halfway around the world I was free to shed my persona as a simple housewife from California. I could create any back story I wanted for myself. This was going to be fun.

Two days later, I arrived in Sorrento, Italy, as seasoned solo traveler flush with independence. I dined at tables for one in sidewalk cafes, shopped for hand-painted dishes in the seaside town of Positano and immersed myself in the local culture. I visited olive oil presses, wineries and chocolate shops. Between tours of the ruins of Pompeii and island of Capri I feasted on pasta and gelato until I feared none of my clothes would ever fit again.

But most of all I cooked. Alongside two of Italy's most famous chefs, I created scialatielli with provola cheese, eggplant, and tomato. I braised red snapper and nestled it in a rich Mediterranean sauce of tomatoes, olives, and peppers. I rolled out succulent pillows of gnocchi, standing elbow to elbow with culinary masters, understanding only a word here and there in the torrent of Italian that flowed continuously as we worked. We didn't need to speak the same language: our hands did the talking. Never have I experienced such ecstasy in a kitchen. It was my version of nirvana.

Upon arriving home I prepared a five-course Italian dinner for forty friends. Our limited number of chairs and tableware required that guests choose between an early afternoon and a late evening seating. In a shocking display of overconfidence, I actually pulled off back-to-back dinner parties. At each guest's place at the table sat one of the scores of tiny bottles of hand-pressed olive oil I had hauled all the way from Sorrento. I roasted two whole salmon, each layered with thinly sliced potatoes to resemble fish scales. My kitchen looked like it had been crop-dusted with flour after I finished rolling and cutting the mountains of gnocchi, served with a rich gorgonzola sauce, as the second course of the meal. I created three flavors of gelato for a grand finale.

After all of that, a dinner for eight would be no more strenuous than a stroll around the Sonoma plaza.

But just because I had the guts - or lack of sanity - to take on such a task didn't explain why I was willing to exert so much effort in the kitchen. What is it about the act of combining ingredients while standing over a stove that appeals to me so much? Is it genetics or something more essential and distinctively characteristic of who I am? In the unique landscape of my mind are imagination and sautéing located in the same cluster of brain cells?

For most people cooking is simply a household chore, a necessity of existence. But in my life, as with other avowed "foodies," cooking had far transcended that meager role to become something much more meaningful. A friend once theorized that if I were ever stranded on a deserted island, one of the first things I'd do would be to go in search of something to cook. He's probably right.

I come from a long line of superb cooks. My maternal grandmother was Ukrainian and worked for many years as a chef. Incredibly she had no sense of smell, having lost it when she nearly died during the flu epidemic of the early 1900s. But she was a master in the kitchen, never consulting a recipe; she simply relied on her years of innate culinary knowledge to create delectable meals. Some of my fondest memories include being in the kitchen with her and my aunts as they sang, laughed uproariously and danced around the stove in their flower-print dresses and aprons. Between shots of vodka they somehow managed to produce the most mouth-watering borscht and stuffed cabbage rolls you've ever tasted. These large-breasted, boisterous women would swallow me up in their arms, engulfing me in a powerful blend of garlic, alcohol and drugstore perfume. Joining them in the kitchen was a privilege allotted only to the girls in the family. Unlike my brother and all my male cousins, I did not have to obey the command to "go outside and play." I could stay with the women and revel in that heady atmosphere of feminine solidarity. It was the best imaginable benefit of being female. I was nearly a grown woman before I realized men were sometimes permitted in kitchens, too.

As a small child I was only allowed to do the most simple of tasks - shelling peas and peeling carrots - but I dreamed of the day when I could stand at the stove. My mother was also an excellent cook and encouraged me to learn when I was in my early teens. By the time I was in my twenties, I had taken many classes, including one on bread-making from James Beard. At that age I was too naïve to realize I was cooking next to a legend. He was just an amiable old bald guy who taught me how to knead properly.

Oddly enough, when I was in my early twenties and married to my first husband, in spite of all the training I had received, I did not consider myself a good cook. Nor did he deem me capable of creating anything but the most pedestrian of dishes. And he knew everything. A small inner voice told me he might be wrong, but that voice was drowned out by a much more insistent one that always sided with him. After all, which of us was the better judge of my many shortcomings: me or the guy with the college degree, a command of trivia that would impress a "Jeopardy" champion and a steady paycheck? It took me seventeen years to recognize some important truths: a bachelor's degree in zoology does not prove you are smarter than I am, a ready supply of useless facts does not make you an expert on anything, and money is one of the least effective means of assessing your self-worth. When I woke up to that reality, I realized I was capable of being much more than just his wife and set out to discover my store of hidden talents, sans my smarty-pants of a spouse.

Nevertheless, so faint was the voice telling me I'd find self-respect in the kitchen that I didn't hear it until I was well into my forties. I knew I loved the sensations I experienced cooking, even that aching cold of diving your hand into a bowl of raw meat to work in the spices, or the sharp eye-sting of freshly chopped onion. Filling the house with the yeasty aroma of baking bread had always been a deeply gratifying experience. Although I had often stumbled in my attempts to develop a career for myself, I always felt at home in a kitchen. However, I had never considered myself anything but a mediocre preparer of meals, an ordinary housewife who could get a passable dinner on the table.

In truth, I was a damned fine cook who had just never heard the applause of an appreciative audience. After my divorce, with no one to cook for and little confidence in my abilities, it was not surprising that my inner chef was unappreciated and under-utilized.

Having grown up with a disabled mother, Michael had little exposure to home-cooked meals. In fact, his nickname as a kid was "Mal," as in malnutrition. He and his brother enjoyed an actual cooked meal only on the rare occasions when a neighbor or friend would drop by with a casserole. The vast, multicourse Italian meal he enjoyed at his grandmother's house made Sundays his favorite day of the week.

During his short-lived first marriage, gourmet cooking was not the focus of the family either. With their two small sons born only fifteen months apart, his wife could hardly be faulted for her lack of culinary creativity. By the time we met, Michael had been subsisting on bachelor fare for nearly ten years. I could have slapped together a baloney sandwich and he would have thought it was a decent meal.

I knew he loved my long legs and my hearty laugh, and he was well aware of the effect his Aegean sea-blue eyes had on me. But in reality, it was for much more profound reasons we had gravitated toward one another. He had a deep, unfilled desire to be nurtured.

I desperately needed to be valued. Food proved to be the means through which we healed one another. Each lovingly prepared meal I placed in front of him came from my heart, and he never failed to be deeply grateful for my gift. With an appreciative and complimentary partner, I finally got to enjoy the sound of an ovation. That encouragement was all I needed to delve into my wealth of culinary talents. At first a customer base of one was all I needed to persuade me to dust off my cookbooks and attempt increasingly complicated recipes. As time went on, a larger stage beckoned.

It wasn't just Michael's encouragement that drew me into the kitchen; I have always felt there is something very fulfilling about providing food to another person. It is, in fact, the first display of human kindness that most of us encounter entering this world. Providing nourishment to another is a profoundly generous act. But when you attempt to elevate the meal beyond simple sustenance to a sensory event, eating becomes an experience that can feed the soul as well as the body.

And then there is the sheer artistry of cooking. With a palate of spices and a canvas of fresh vegetables, meats and pasta, the challenge is to create something that appeals to as many of the senses as possible. That silky sensation of a delicate panne cotta, the intoxicating aroma of a simmering sauce, a fresh salad bursting with the colors of summer and, of course, the amazing dance of the taste buds are all choreographed by the cook. A meal can be a simple sketch or a grand masterpiece, but each one represents another opportunity to express a creative urge.

But perhaps the core of my passion lies purely in the setting. Kitchens have always been my sanctuaries, places to escape from turmoil and frustration. I can nearly always ignore aggravations with the aroma of spices and bubbling soups, a warm oven, and the joy of banging around my pots and pans. I love the organization of my kitchen. While nearly every other aspect of my life ranges from a bit untidy to downright chaotic, my kitchen remains steadfastly efficient and meticulously ordered. I brook no carelessness in the arrangement of its contents. Friends think I'm being polite when I wave them from my kitchen, refusing their assistance in preparing a meal. The truth is that I hate the thought of anyone rummaging around in my fastidiously arranged utensils and ingredients.

"You are a very graceful cook, you know," a friend once observed while I shifted from one work surface to the next, grilling a ham and gruyere panini for her, tearing up the salad greens and tossing them with pears and rosemary pecans, squeezing a lemon into the dressing, and reaching for a plate from the shelf.

"Graceful" was not a term often applied to me after I contracted Multiple Sclerosis.

But in my postage stamp of a kitchen, with a counter to steady myself always within easy reach, I actually did feel quite fluid, even agile. I knew every inch of this diminutive workspace. I could reach out and grasp the cool, slightly slippery bottle of olive oil that sits to the right of my stove without even glancing at it. The smoked paprika is in the second drawer on the left, third row, first bottle on the right. My mandolin, with its wickedly sharp blades, rests harmlessly in the narrow cupboard next to the dishwasher. There is always fresh-churned butter in the door of the refrigerator from the creamery over on Second Street East. Mixing bowls and platters of every size sit on the wire shelves that line one wall, right next to the bread flour and raw sugar.

This is my turf. It is the one place in the world where I feel powerful and in control. It is both very achingly familiar and reassuringly predictable. Simply put, the chemistry of cooking and the harmony of my kitchen make sense to me, even when the rest of the world is so damned unruly.

*At every party there are two kinds of people: those who want to go home and those who don't. The trouble is, they are usually married to each other.*

**~Ann Landers**

*two*

If I was going to continue with this little adventure of mine, I was going to need guests—a lot of them. Our core group consisted of only about fifty friends and family members. To accomplish my goal of having a full table each week, I would need over three hundred people to say yes to an invitation. I couldn't even name that many people, much less invite them to a party.

"Do you know anyone else who might like to come to dinner, Michael?"

"Maybe, but we need to talk about this. Exactly how many people do you plan on feeding?"

"Well, I was thinking six guests each week would be nice."

"For fifty-two weeks?" His eyes were narrowing as he added up the numbers. I had to talk fast before he could finish doing the math.

"But I'm sure a lot of people will join us on more than one Sunday, so I really won't need a whole bunch of people on the guest list."

"I have a feeling your idea of what constitutes a whole bunch is a lot different than mine. Do I get any say about who is on this list?"

"Sure. In fact, why don't you take charge of issuing invitations? Whenever you meet someone interesting, you can ask them if they would like to come to one of our dinners. It'll be fun." I had to work at keeping my voice slightly languid. He can spot a cheery, flippant tone as a hard sell every time.

The corners of his mouth involuntarily turned up. Michael is a man who enjoys people. He will breezily chat up even the most lifeless person in a room. And I'd just given him permission to bring that guy home for dinner. It was a risky move, but I was desperate.

"I can ask anyone?"

"Of course," I gulped. "I'll invite people I meet, too." If I worked fast, I was certain I could supply at least a couple of animated guests each Sunday.

So our plan was hatched. When either of us met someone we found interesting, we would invite that person to dinner. However, we both discovered that an invitation delivered within fifteen minutes of having been introduced to someone wasn't always received with enthusiasm. Some invitees were skeptical (what are you selling?), others were incredulous (I don't even know you!) and still others were even somewhat apprehensive (you don't look like a con-artist).

Thankfully, most people took us up on the offer, though. In addition, our innovative means of finding interesting guests through chance encounters was proving to be one of the most amusing aspects of our adventure.

After having spent three years in Tennessee, my ears can detect a Southern accent over the din of a crowd, or above the clamor in the aisles of a grocery store. I was shopping for Sunday's dinner when I heard a drawl as thick as grits and gravy.

"Don't ya'll have any yella rice? I've looked everywhere and I can't find it."

The clerk was obviously confused by the request, but charmed silly by the glamorous woman before him. He was on his hands and knees earnestly searching the bottom shelves in a sincere attempt to assist her.

I love Southern women. They are able to cloak a formidable degree of tenacity with a veil of graciousness that leaves most men completely defenseless. You don't control a Southern woman; you just get out of her way.

"They call it saffron rice here in the North," I pitched in. It didn't matter that we were as far west as you could get on the continent. I learned in Nashville that anyone who lives outside of the Deep South is a Northerner.

"Well, bless your heart. Thank you. Here it is right in front of me."

After that brief exchange, Dee and I went on to discuss everything we missed about Tennessee, while fellow shoppers maneuvered their carts around us. And of course, I invited her to dinner. I never pass up the opportunity to become friends with a Southern woman.

Our goal was to connect with others through good food and wine. Evidently, that sounded like a damned fine objective to a lot of people. What's more, many told us they had not been invited to someone else's home for dinner in years. They were thrilled to be included on our guest list.

Before we knew it we had over one hundred people vying for a seat at our table.

## Menu:

*Naples-style pizza*
with four cheeses

*Lemon risotto*
with asparagus & scallops

*Field greens*
with blood orange vinaigrette

*Individual olive oil cakes*
drizzled with orange marmalade

## Guest List:

Sandi & Fred
Rebecca & Dave
Karin & Susan

Only our second dinner, and we already had the makings of a disaster with thrills, spills, and lost friends wandering the mean streets of Sonoma.

Nearly all of our guests were former neighbors with whom we've shared a cul-de-sac or a condo complex. These were the people I could count on when I needed a cup of flour or a shoulder to cry on.

Perhaps forgetting that we no longer lived just steps from their door, two of our friends had decided to walk to our new house. As the rest of us were starting on our second glass of wine, we began to worry about them. Then the phone rang. They had overshot our street by about a mile and were lost out in the Sonoma countryside. Michael took off in the car and found them by the side of the road next to a pasture of slightly confused cows. He delivered them safely to the house before all the appetizers were gone.

During the meal, we recalled lots of memories and told many stories. Although the art of storytelling is nearly lost, around a dinner table is one place to revive it, especially when everyone is savoring that last glass of wine.

We laughed at Rebecca's account of huddling in a bathtub during a tornado in Oklahoma and fussing at her husband for refusing to join her. David provided the punch line by adding that the tub was located directly under a skylight.

The real comedic moments of the evening, however, occurred before the guests even arrived. I have always cooked my pizzas on the grill with a pizza stone. As it was too chilly to stand outside in front of the barbeque, I decided to bake the pizza in the oven instead. Unfortunately, some of the cheese spilled and caught fire, producing just enough smoke to set off the alarm. With the piercing screech growing more insistent, pandemonium ensued. Michael furiously flapped a towel at the smoke alarm while trying to shout instructions over the racket. Bella was whining pitifully and running in circles, while I scurried from room to room opening the doors and windows. Nevertheless, the shrill blast continued to reverberate throughout the house. The ear-piercing shriek of the alarm stopped only seconds before the doorbell rang. If our guests heard the commotion while approaching the front door, or wondered why their hosts were panting with exhaustion, they politely refrained from asking any questions.

Two dinners, somewhat ineptly accomplished, only fifty more to go. If I could avoid burning down the house, I might just pull this off.

Despite the minor mishaps, we were having a great time with my innovative MS remedy and our friends seemed to be enjoying the therapy as well. For those who joined our guest list, a room full of lively conversation, some good food, and a nice glass of wine were just an e-mail away.

Even so, we were turned down by a few people. After talking with a neighbor who had repeatedly declined our invitations, I learned that the perceived obligation to reciprocate was the reason. For some, the thought of inviting others to their home for a dinner party was enough to send them into a tizzy. Even our assurance that we didn't expect an invitation in return was not enough to entice these people to join us.

But one person's rejection of my invitations cut me to the quick. Kathy and I had been friends from our days as young mothers living in the suburbs. We had seen one another through painful divorces, agonized over the antics of our unruly teenagers and even planned the cruises we would take together in our retirement years. Her recent marriage, however, had driven a wedge between us. Previously, we had never let anyone, including spouses, come between us. Our first husbands had little in common so we just enjoyed adventures without them. We scrounged garage sales on weekends, nearly ruined each other's hair with home perms and took in all the "chick flicks" together. Over nearly twenty years of friendship we consumed gallons of coffee while sorting out the frustrations and complexities of life.

And we always had each other's back. I will never forget the time Kathy saved my reputation as a hostess. I had asked a young couple over for dinner and somehow completely forgot about the invitation. When my doorbell rang on the appointed evening and I found two nicely dressed people standing on my front porch, smiling widely, I felt the color drain from my face. Not only was my house littered with toys but all I had for dinner was a very plain beef stew. They were vegetarians. While I frantically fished all the meat out of the stew, Kathy slipped over and handed a beautiful salad over my back fence. That's the kind of friends we were.

If I couldn't entice her to come with her new husband I'd just have to plan a "girls' night out" dinner. It was unimaginable that my year of dinner parties would fail to include at least one evening with my best friend.

Although I missed Kathy's company, our guest list was beginning to include some fascinating new friends. Most of the people we invited were of our own ilk: outgoing party lovers who were happy to meet new friends and have some laughs. But not every guest was a good fit. It became clear that a couple of people viewed our home as little more than an upscale soup kitchen. Not that anything was required, but social etiquette dictates that when invited to someone's home for dinner, you bring along a nice bottle of wine to share or maybe a bouquet of flowers. Even a small jar of homemade jam was a welcomed gift. What you don't bring is an extra guest or a plastic-lined purse. We actually had one woman who, when she thought no one was watching, shoveled a plate of gnocchi in her handbag. Her name got crossed off the list the next morning.

Showing up late was another way to get removed from the list. I have always held the belief that a host expects me within twenty minutes of the time stated on the dinner invitation; his or her efforts in the kitchen warrant the courtesy of promptness. When I am the host, nothing gets me tapping my foot in frustration faster than trying to keep a meal warm while we wait on a straggler. There's nothing fashionable about sauntering in forty minutes late to dinner without a good excuse.

Fortunately, most people were courteous and considerate. We also discovered our guests to be well-mannered when seated next to someone with an opinion that differed from theirs. While we weren't putting soapboxes in place of chairs around the table, we also weren't attempting to steer our guests away from lively debates. In fact, we openly encouraged conversations between opposing sides on the socially taboo topics of politics and religion. Because we didn't attempt to orchestrate the grouping of guests—it was strictly first-come, first-served—we never knew what the mix might be. Our black, lesbian friends might be seated next to an evangelical Christian couple. A liberal feminist might find herself across the table from a staunch Republican. Needless to say, the combinations made for some very riveting dinner conversations.

It was amazing that we didn't have any serious dust-ups at the table. I believe the tone of our dinners was influenced by an awareness that my days as a hostess might end soon. Although the subject of my illness was rarely discussed, everyone knew the impetus for our dinner parties. It was, perhaps, an underlying factor in the level of civility displayed. Or maybe everyone simply recognized that, in spite of our differences, we are all just trying to find the joy in life while we still have the capacity to appreciate it.

When someone suggested that our experience would make a great reality show, I pointed out that the only way it would be a success is if the evenings ended in food fights. Fortunately, reality shows aside, few people are willing to ruin a nice dinner by being offensive. A raucous, ill-mannered party might make for riveting television fare, but rudeness is not all that entertaining when experienced firsthand.

As it turned out, it was a simple piece of furniture that would ultimately define the mood of our dinners. A decorator friend had politely pointed out that the old, nicked-up rectangular table we had wedged awkwardly into our dining room was not befitting our events. She suggested that a square table would be more proportionate to the space.

While searching for such an item, I learned they were referred to in the furniture trade as "gathering tables." Perfect. Not only did a large, square table offer a more democratic forum for our lively discussions, with all guests facing one another, but it gave us a new name for our affairs. We'd ditch the stuffy title of "dinner party" and go with the much more approachable designation of "gathering."

Finding a gathering table that would fit into my budget and into our diminutive dining room had proven to be a formidable task requiring weeks of searching Internet want ads. It had to be a specific style, height, and dimension. I thought I had a clear vision of how this particular decorating dilemma was to be solved, but meticulously measuring the space, even to the point of taping out a proposed location for the table, did not prepare me for the sight of the massive, four-legged brute that now squatted in my home. It was a beast of a table.

I had been forced to drag one burly leg at a time into the house and then round up a team of neighbors to hoist the top off of the delivery truck and into my dining room. Assembling it exhausted us all. A dainty flower arrangement in the middle of the table and the placement of my upholstered chairs did little to minimize its overpowering presence. Considering the herculean effort required to wrestle it into place, I resolved to live with it. If it ever left my dining room, it would have to go out on its own steam.

At its inaugural gathering, though, I recognized the giant table's congenial nature. With two guests positioned on each of its four sides the table drew us together and encouraged all to participate in the flow of conversation. Like our ancestors who had banded as one around the safe haven of a campfire, we found ourselves congregating around this hospitable table in a circle of camaraderie.

The table became cemented into place as the aroma from scores of meals slowly seeped into its grain and the weight of countless elbows gradually pressed it deeper into the floor. In time it would be elevated to the status of a family heirloom in the making, a symbol of my triumph. Someday my sons would have the privilege of grappling with the beast.

# Menu:

**Kalamata olives,**
rosemary almonds and
cave-aged Gouda

**San Francisco-style Cioppino**
with warm artisan breadsticks

**Classic Caesar salad**

**Warm Panettone bread**
**pudding**
with homemade custard gelato

## Guest list:

Chip & Jeanne
John & Dorothy
Ed & Maggie
Konrad

Only three weeks into this challenge and I was already beginning to rethink the entire plan. It was a crazy idea anyway. Severe fatigue had been plaguing me for several days and I just wanted to dump myself on the couch in front of the television. A party was last on the list of appealing options. I was mulling over a suitable excuse when Sunday morning arrived, rainy and gray. Calling all of our guests and bowing out would only add to the bleakness of the day and drop me further into a state of gloom.

Michael offered to do the shopping and I decided to scale back on several dishes. With a little resolve and a can of Red Bull, I decided I could soldier on. Thankfully, the complexities of cooking consumed my thoughts and allowed me to ignore the sensation that I was trudging through mud as I prepared the meal. When our guests arrived I had the appetizers out and a smile planted on my face. I'm certain they didn't realize I was struggling just to stay upright. As a veteran of the MS game, my friend Jeanne, however, had a clue. She also knew to say nothing. I certainly didn't want my guests guilt-ridden by the effort I'd put forth to feed them.

Ed and Maggie, our former neighbors from across town, were joining us. They were both in their late eighties and grappling with serious health problems of their own, but they had gamely accepted our invitation. If they could buck up for an evening of socializing, so could I.

We had a late addition, as well. Our friend from Nashville had called to tell us that her son would soon be moving from San Francisco to Chicago. She hoped we might be able to include him in one of our dinners before he left the area. I had to add a few extra ingredients to the Cioppino, and the seating at the table was a little snug, but these small accommodations proved well worth the effort. This young man, at age twenty-three, was knowledgeable and well-spoken. He was also aware of the advantages he enjoyed in life. His parents had been imprisoned during the Solidarity movement in Poland and had sacrificed greatly to make their way to America.

The ages of our guests spanned nearly seven decades and allowed for a fascinating flow of conversation, with our young guest providing insight into his generation's view on a variety of social and political issues and our more mature guests offering the perspective of their years. It was touching to listen to them council him on career paths and life choices—and even more heartwarming to realize how thoroughly appreciative he was of their advice.

It was becoming obvious that this adventure of ours was not just about the food. It was about bringing people together. The meal was simply the backdrop for the gathering of a variety of engaging, remarkable people. And from the smiles and laughter of our friends, it seemed that our concept was being well received.

Bella, our standard poodle, was also enjoying the rotating crop of potential ear-scratchers. She worked every new roomful of people like a politician on a campaign sweep through Iowa. Every guest got the opportunity to pet her, and if anyone missed a chance, Bella gently placed a paw on his or her lap as a reminder of the hospitality she offered. While most of our friends would have trouble remembering the names of our four adult children, all are thoroughly enamored of Bella.

There is no creature more loving and gentle than Bella. We've often joked that Bella is the reincarnation of a Buddhist monk. Her meditative state might look a lot like sleep, but we're convinced she's got something deep going on inside her furry head.

I grew up with dogs, along with a virtual zoo of various creatures my brother and I carted home. We even had a pet squirrel. Orphaned at only a couple weeks of age, it didn't stand much of a chance at survival until it was brought to my mother. She fed it with an eyedropper and in doing so, she turned a rodent into a loyal companion. I can still picture her in the kitchen washing dishes with that squirrel perched on her shoulder.

Michael, on the other hand, had never lived with an animal of any kind. In a household with a wheelchair-bound mother, two growing boys and a father who was trying to hold down two jobs, a pet would have been just one moving part too many. Having never had any experience with animals, he was certain they posed more trouble than they were worth.

But dogs have always had a special place in my heart, especially poodles. I kept my fingers crossed behind my back when Michael extracted a pledge from me to live pet-free. Then, during a week when he was sailing with his buddy Scott, I went out and bought a six-week-old standard poodle puppy who was to become the third member of our little pack. To say that Michael was less than thrilled would be an understatement. For once, however, I held firm against my Sicilian's rampage. Bella was staying. I knew he'd someday come to realize that he really did need a dog in his life, even though at first he refused to call her by name.

"Ronda, the thing is in here."

"You mean Bella?"

"Whatever. Come and get the thing. It's sitting on my foot."

His resolve didn't last long, though. In a matter of weeks she worked her way onto his lap and into his heart. From then on he was like a convert to religion. No man has loved his dog more, even though Bella might not have been the one he would have selected.

He once told me that when he was a little kid he used to dream about owning a dog. "I knew why we couldn't have one but I always loved shows like *Rin Tin Tin* and *Lassie*, and imagined what great adventures I'd have if I had a dog like that."

"And thanks to me, now you do!"

"Not exactly. I never once pictured myself owning a poodle, much less one the size of a Shetland pony."

There is no truer example of a man confident in his masculinity than one who will stroll the aisles of a hardware store with an enormous poodle at his side.

## Menu:

*Homemade ricotta*
with warm artisan bread

*Rabbit Ragu*
over handmade rosemary
fettuccini noodles

*Fresh greens*
with candied pecans
and balsamic vinaigrette

*Meyers Lemon
Budino*
with crème fraiche

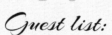

## Guest list:

Susan & Alan
Alexandra & MaryJane
Jean & Doug

Once again I chose a rather elaborate main course. I couldn't help myself. I had found a rabbit ragu recipe similar to a dish I had recently enjoyed at Michael Chiarello's restaurant in Yountville, California. Unfortunately, it involved a lot of prep work and time over the stove and I also had to push past my squeamishness over cooking Thumper. First, however, I had to find a source for fresh rabbit. I had never seen it advertised in the grocery flyers and I certainly wasn't going to head off, Elmer Fudd-like, into the local fields with a shotgun.

Frank is the butcher at a marvelous little grocery store in town named Sonoma Market. An affable Italian with a huge smile, he always greets his customers with a boisterous bellow across the meat counter. As the year progressed, my rabbit ragu became our guests' favorite dish and one I made often. Not many of Frank's customers requested whole rabbits, boned out, but he always kept a few bunnies in his meat locker and was only too glad to ready one for my Sunday dinner. Over time he began to refer to me as "The Rabbit Lady." I never bothered to offer my real name. I grew to love being greeted with the loud announcement, "Hey, it's the Rabbit Lady! What are you cooking this week, doll?"

The ricotta, however, was my favorite dish to prepare. As I learned from Chef Chiarello, making homemade ricotta is incredibly easy. All you need is a large pot, a square of cheesecloth, a colander and a slotted spoon. In the pot, mix half a gallon of whole milk with two cups of cream. Dissolve a tablespoon of salt in two cups of filtered or bottled water and add to the mixture. Slowly bring it all to a boil. Then quickly turn off the heat and add a third cup of freshly squeezed lemon juice and a teaspoon of grated lemon peel. The citrus will cause curds to form. Allow the mixture to rest for a few minutes before gently scooping the curds with a slotted spoon into a cheesecloth-lined colander, discarding the remaining liquid, called "whey." Let the excess liquid drain from the cheese for a few minutes. I then like to layer the cheese in a small casserole dish with either grated parmesan and herbs or maybe even a little fig compote. Serve it alongside a nice loaf of artisan bread and you'll hear a chorus of compliments.

Homemade bread is also remarkably simple when you know a few secrets. All that's required to produce warm, crusty bread and fill your house with mouthwatering aromas are four ingredients and a little patience. Add one and a half tablespoons of yeast and the same amount of salt to three cups of lukewarm water in a large bowl. Mix in six and a half cups of bread flour and stir until there are no dry spots. You will then have a seriously ugly lump of dough. Throw a kitchen towel over it and go watch a couple of hours of HGTV. Five hours is even better. Then shape the dough into two rounded softball-sized mounds. Cut a couple of slits in the top of each loaf, dust them with a little flour and allow them to rest for half an hour or so. In the meantime, preheat your oven to 450 degrees with a pizza or baking stone placed on the middle rack and a broiler pan on the bottom rack. The best means of delivering the bread to your oven is with a pizza paddle sprinkled with cornmeal. After you've positioned your loaves on the stone, toss a cup of warm water into the broiler pan, quickly closing the door to retain the steam. In just about thirty minutes you'll have gorgeous, golden loaves of the crustiest, most delicious bread you've ever tasted. Be prepared to purchase the next size up in jeans: you're going to be eating a lot of bread.

I soon learned that I would have the opportunity to discuss my exploits in the kitchen with the author of my favorite cookbook. A friend had arranged for me and my equally starry-eyed daughter-in-law, Amanda, to meet Michael Chiarello at his Yountville restaurant, Bottega. My husband wisely chose to stay at home for this adventure, offering to babysit our grandson, Jack.

"Don't you want to go with us, Michael?"

"With you and Amanda drooling all over some handsome Italian chef? I think I'll just let Jack drool on me instead while I watch the football game. Just bring home a doggie bag of pasta for me."

When introduced to Chef Chiarello, I boldly told him about our Sunday dinners and then offered to send him an invitation. He gave me his e-mail address and said he'd be honored to attend if he could work it into his schedule. Then the panic set in. What if he actually showed up and I got so nervous I totally blew the dinner, making a complete ass of myself in front of a famous chef? Oh well, I rationalized, I had made a fool of myself before and lived to tell the tale. I sent the e-mail.

Although invited, Michael Chiarello was never able to come to one of our dinners, but he offered his heartfelt support of my endeavor. His cookbook provided much of the inspiration for my menus, and many of his recipes were favorites that I ended up using time and time again throughout the year. His simple yet elegant take on Italian cuisine dovetailed perfectly with all I had learned in Italy.

That I was willing to invite one of the best-known chefs in the country to my home for dinner demonstrated the ridiculous amount of self-confidence I was developing as a cook. I had brazenly started to feel that no menu was too ambitious, no recipe too difficult to execute perfectly. Audacity is the surest way to tempt fate.

## Menu:

### Homemade ricotta
with freshly baked
artisan bread

### Handmade gnocchi
with sauce Bolognese

### Field greens with
Meyers lemon vinaigrette

### Classic tiramisu

### Guest list:

Barbara & Bob
Mike & Phyllis
John & Shana

I had a feeling it was coming: the night when my luck would run out and chaos would reign in my kitchen. I had become entirely too smug about my ability to create a flawless dinner party. The cooking gods were about to give me a smack-down.

The day began innocently enough. I spent a leisurely morning reading *The New York Times* and then decided to kick it into gear with an hour or so of housecleaning. My first clue that things were amiss was a shredded roll of paper towels. The mystery was solved a few hours later when I reached into a cupboard for a bowl and found mouse droppings. Eek! I am extremely phobic when it comes to mice. Actually any animal with a long, hairless tail gives me the creeps.

I have good reason to hold a low opinion of mice. Due to several bouts of premature labor I was confined to my bed while pregnant with my second son. One afternoon I heard the telltale scratching sounds of a mouse in the bedroom. My ex-husband was sure I was wrong. It was probably just the wind outside. He assured me that even if there was a mouse in the room it was surely more afraid of me than the other way around. I doubted it. Sitting on the edge of the bed I tried to pinpoint the creature's whereabouts. Suddenly I felt a strange sensation running up my spine. The mouse was inside my nightgown! I leaped up on the bed and unleashed a blood-curdling scream while the mouse scurried up and around my armpits and down the front of my extended belly, finally dropping on the floor in front of my astonished husband. Needless to say, I *detest* mice.

The discovery of a mouse in my beloved kitchen required me to wash all of the dishes from the cupboards and sterilize every surface. That put me hours behind schedule. But the worst part was that I had to start cooking knowing that beady little eyes were watching me. Stressed and traumatized, I set out to make the ricotta. Somewhere along the line I did something wrong because the curds did not form. All I had for my efforts were eleven cups of milk, cream, and salt water to pour down the drain. Michael shuffled off to the store for more milk and cream, mumbling, "Why can't we just buy ricotta?"

Fortunately, I had made the meat sauce for the gnocchi earlier and could assemble the tiramisu for dessert while he was gone. Still, by the time he returned, our guests were due in just thirty minutes. I had not changed clothes, combed my hair, or even brushed my teeth. The potatoes for the gnocchi weren't peeled, much less cooked. And I swore I could hear the sound of nasty little feet scampering through my cupboards.

All the while, Bella, pacifist that she is, was resting serenely on the couch. Attacking intruders was not in the job description of a reincarnated monk.

The bread was baked to perfection and just coming out of the oven as everyone arrived. Warm, homemade bread is a great attention-grabber so no one seemed to notice that the hostess was covered in flour and wrestling with a mountain of gnocchi dough. At least I had managed to throw on an apron, fluff my hair and brush my teeth.

Thank goodness the second batch of ricotta was a success. I served it with the bread while Michael kept everyone's wine glass full. None of our guests had been to one of our Sunday dinners, so they didn't seem baffled by the appetizer portion of the evening being stretched out for so long.

My first dozen or so gnocchi were perfect little pillows of potato, eggs, and flour. But after twenty minutes or so of rolling and cutting, I became far less finicky about the aesthetics of my pasta. The last few were downright ugly. What the hell, with enough sauce thrown over them, no one would notice anyway. The salad was supposed to be a Caesar, but I was on the ropes, exhausted and frazzled. Romaine, croutons, grated parmesan and vinaigrette would have to do.

If they sensed the mayhem occurring in the kitchen, our guests politely refrained from comments. Michael jump-started the conversation with his question for the evening: "What was the funniest moment of your life?" The laughter from the living room kept me from ripping off my apron and calling the pizza delivery boy. At least some of us were having fun.

The platter full of gnocchi finally reached the table to a chorus of oohs and ahhs, and after I had calmed my nerves with a few glasses of wine, I realized I had made a fuss over nothing. Our friends weren't the least bit concerned by the belated arrival of the main course, nor were they bothered by my slightly disheveled appearance. To all of them it was simply a fabulous evening of belly laughs, camaraderie and great food. Who cares about a silly little mouse?

By the time everyone had been escorted to the door I was soothed enough to gaze upon the mountain of dirty dishes and just walk away. They'd all get washed soon enough. The mouse could have one last, great night on earth before he met an untimely end.

The next morning, however, as Michael recalled my struggles in the kitchen and the sight of tears cutting a path down my flour-dusted face, he stated that he was ready to throw in the towel on this ludicrous plan of ours.

"You know that stress can cause a flare-up. Why are we doing this?"

"Because I need to. Besides, all the trouble was the mouse's fault."

"You know, everything would be a lot easier if you'd simplify these dinners. Just make burgers or something."

"I'm not going to serve hamburgers every week."

"What are you going to do to then?"

"Kill that mouse."

"Fine. I think we have some traps in the garage. I'll get them for you."

"You're the Sicilian in the family. I think you should handle anything that involves death."

"Absolutely right. I'm on it." No Italian man can resist the opportunity for a little revenge.

Actually I did recognize the logic of his argument about simplifying the menus, but I wasn't going to revert to preparing frat party fare for my dinners. One idea was to start serving the food family-style. I had an enormous platter that Michael had given me for one of our anniversaries. Rimming the plate is one of my favorite sayings, "One cannot sleep well, love well, or live well unless one has dined well." I reasoned that it would be a lot easier to utilize it for nearly the entire meal than to continue schlepping one plated course after the other to the table. Plus, this would give me more opportunity to participate in the fascinating conversations buzzing around the table.

After that day, nearly every dinner was served on my beautiful platter, which I placed in the center of the table. The salad course was also served in one huge bowl with guests helping themselves while passing the bread and olive oil around the table. This arrangement proved to be much less snobbish than the four-course meals I had been slaving to get to the table and enhanced the tone of togetherness and informality that we had hoped to achieve.

We had started this endeavor because I wanted to cook and spend time with friends. Because cooking is such an obsession, I initially focused on the food, but over time, we came to the conclusion that the menu wasn't all that important. It was the companionship, pure and simple. That and a nice glass of chardonnay.

But just switching to family-style dining was not an infallible means of avoiding flare-ups. Stress, heat, and over-exertion were all common triggers. Sometimes it was hard to predict what might bring on a bout of misery.

Not knowing what is coming at you next is the most frustrating aspect of dealing with MS. Some days you feel just fine. In fact, many people go for months or even years without MS putting much of a crimp in their lifestyle—only to have it return with a vengeance when least expected.

There are actually several types of MS. The most common, relapsing-remitting, was the verdict I received. It is characterized by unpredictable attacks or relapses followed by periods of remission. Often within about ten years of living with the disease, you transition to secondary progressive, a stage in which you slowly lose mobility and sensation with few, if any, periods of remissions. Finally, there's Primary Progressive MS, the most severe type and the diagnosis Michael's mother received. She just declined, with no periods of remission, losing her ability to walk, control of her bladder, and eventually her ability to fight off infection. She lived for decades trapped in a body that became uncontrollable in a measured and irreversible march downward.

It is rare to contract MS after age fifty. From what I read late-onset MS tends to progress a little faster as well. One study I found online projected a lifespan of a mere sixteen years after diagnosis. With two down, fourteen more did not seem nearly enough. But I was even more apprehensive about what those years might look like.

With a lot of soul-searching and long talks with Michael, as well as some afternoon chats with my friend Jeanne I was able to wrap my head around the idea of life in a wheelchair.

As is common with MS, Jeanne contracted the disease in her early thirties and lived with it for over a decade before her mobility was compromised. However, with her motorized scooter and walker, she now enjoys a full and rich life in our little town. She is a constant presence at wine events, parties, and club meetings throughout the community. Her engaging personality, warm smile, and positive attitude encourage everyone to seek out her friendship. With a fashion model's figure and sense of style, she turns heads in spite of her disability not because of it.

Watching her build a fulfilling life with this disease gave me hope. I fully expected my future challenges to be similar to hers and felt that, through Jeanne, I had a roadmap for this journey. But MS is a strange disease in that different people can experience dissimilar sets of symptoms. In my extensive reading I learned that for most people the primary issues are balance, mobility and loss of sensation. For some, however, chronic pain is their cross to bear.

I was alone in the house when I suffered my first "MS hug," a far-too-benevolent term for such an unbearably painful experience. While sitting at my desk, I suddenly felt as though my chest was being squeezed so tightly I couldn't inhale another breath. *"Oh, hell, I'm about to die of a heart attack"* was my first thought. I was exactly the same age as my father had been when he keeled over from a sudden heart stoppage. Of course, he weighed nearly three hundred pounds and had tortured his body with cigarette smoke for forty years. Still, the notion that genetics might be handing me the same fate, in spite of my good health habits, caused me to freeze in panic.

No one had ever mentioned that MS could cause such crushing pain. It didn't even occur to me that what was happening was yet another round of artillery fire from my immune system. Foolishly, but true to form, I did not call 9-1-1. I was too scared to move a muscle anyway.

After twenty minutes or so the pain eased up a bit and I called the advice nurse. She put me through to my neurologist who explained that this type of pain was in fact yet another "fascinating" symptom of the disease. It even had a name, *dysesthesias*. A form of neuropathic pain, dysesthesias is a tough nut to crack. It comes and goes with little warning and responds to pain medication only some of the time. That leaves plenty of room for suffering.

Chronic neuropathic pain is an obnoxious companion, wearing you down in its persistence. It shoves everything else in your life aside and takes over. In late summer and throughout the remainder of the year it became an increasingly irritating presence. In addition, debilitating headaches that lasted for weeks were added to the intermittent bouts of dysesthesias. The episodes were becoming increasingly severe and even heavy-duty pain meds no longer provided much of a reprieve. In fact, they actually added to my grief by causing nausea and vomiting. Now, when the pain became simply too much to endure, the only relief was a trip to the emergency room for IV Dilaudid, a morphine derivative. About every four to six weeks Michael rushed me to the hospital. As I writhed in agony, all he could do was hold my hand as we waited for the drug to make its way through my veins with instructions for my whacked out nervous system to draw down the weapons. We were a pitiful pair.

The most frustrating aspect of neuropathic pain is that it is not real. There has been no injury; your damaged nerves just think one has occurred. You can ice a bruised muscle, elevate a swollen limb or bandage a wound, but neuropathic pain is an enemy that won't be placated so easily. Most pain medications are essentially useless. Except one. For the near daily attacks of pain, nothing could beat back the beast as effectively as medical marijuana. Of course it didn't stand a chance in battle against the more severe pain episodes, but at least I could get some relief from the day-to-day torture between ER visits.

Back in my college days, like so many other Baby Boomers, I smoked pot. But when I married my first husband and gave birth to my sons, I left those wild ways behind. Now here I was a grandmother, and I was getting stoned again. Actually getting stoned was not the goal. I wanted relief from the pain, but I didn't want to spend my days lolling on the couch eating chocolate-chip cookie dough. It took a few weeks to gauge just how much marijuana it would take to manage my discomfort but not cause me to behave like a character from a *Cheech and Chong* movie. Those were interesting weeks. Eventually, though, I re-learned how to roll a joint, mask the sweet, earthy aroma of marijuana smoke, and stay away from the Doritos.

While it was now the most debilitating symptom, pain was by no means the only way MS made its presence known. Neurological symptoms can run the gamut from merely annoying to downright bizarre and frightening. When nerve endings transport erroneous messages to your brain your mind issues outlandish commands that the rest of the body nonetheless obeys. It is like finding yourself suddenly inhabiting a land where the king is stark-raving mad.

The onset of my neurological damage was a seemingly innocuous tingling under my chin that quickly deteriorated in the course of twenty-four hours to partial paralysis, loss of sensation, severe balance issues and ultimately, chronic pain. But those broad terms didn't address the myriad of deeply unsettling nerve damage indicators that cropped up daily.

One of the oddest sensations occurred when my rearranged circuitry communicated the very strange news that my feet had become encased in bubble wrap. I literally could not feel my feet touching the ground yet there was a distinct sense something soft and cushy was wrapped around them. Walking became an amusing endeavor. Much to my amazement I learned it is not an uncommon symptom either. Evidently there are legions of us walking around on spongy cushions of plastic.

Another disconcerting development was the migrating numbness that roamed continuously from one part of my body to the next. For hours, sometimes days, a switch would flip off in one area or another. Suddenly it felt as though my right shoulder, upper lip or perhaps my left hand had been painlessly lopped off. These areas ceased to exist as far as my nervous system was concerned. I didn't lose control over my limbs; they were just randomly and temporarily shunned by my obstinate immune system.

After living with MS for a year or so, however, I began to adjust to my strange new body. L'Hermitte's syndrome was a constant source of amusement in a perverse sort of way. Even though I acquired the habit of turning my head in a slow and deliberate fashion, I still would occasionally forget and cause an eerie electrical shock sensation to race up my spine.

Another aspect of my finely tuned nervous system was impossible to ignore: I called it the "tuning fork" effect. Imagine the fast vibrations of a struck tuning fork humming from the tip of your toes to the top of your head. Or better yet, the next time you are at an airport find one of those recliners offering a mechanical massage for a quarter, put in a handful and sit down for an hour or so. Then try walking to your gate.

Once I got over the creepiness of it all, however, I started to appreciate some of what was happening. My body had become hypersensitive to the slightest stimulus. My nerve endings were constantly on red alert, ready to react in a fashion that was beginning to seem normal for me. It was becoming more and more difficult to conjure up memories of the old me. No longer did it feel strange to have a variety of sensations occurring throughout the day. In fact, with the exception of pain, I hardly noticed most of them. At some point I began to grudgingly accept this new body of mine. Instead of freaking out about my out-of-whack neurological system, I started to relax and just go with it. When I considered my new hyper-awareness as a talent of sorts, I began to think of MS as something other than a curse, my heightened sensitivity as my own quirky super power.

That mindset worked to a degree, but when the pain came back I simply wanted to be done with all of this nonsense.

Pain was definitely not something I would have agreed to. I have never been the stoic type. Whining miserably over the slightest injury is more my style. And I certainly would have never copped such a good attitude going into this whole mess if I had known MS was going to hurt. Up to this point I had accepted nearly everything thrown at me with at least a moderate level of grace and maturity, two traits I hadn't shown many signs of in the past. But with the burden of chronic pain added to the mix, I was certain my days as a trooper were over. Nobody was going to think highly of an irritable, weepy woman who did nothing but bitch and moan about her lousy lot in life.

I learned early on, however, that people expect you to buck up and present a brave front. Shortly after I was diagnosed with the disease, Michael and I were invited to a party. I had just come home from the hospital and was still very unsteady on my feet. A woman I didn't know approached me as I used my walker to navigate through the crowd in the living room. She informed me that I was an inspiration. Evidently all I had to do to arouse such high regard was not cry in the corner or fall on my ass.

She wouldn't be so inspired by me now, though. All of the admiration and attention had been, I must admit, rather agreeable. And all I'd had to put up with was a little numbness, wobbly legs, and a few odd sensations to receive it. This pain stuff, on the other hand, was a whole different enchilada. Everyone could just take their nice casseroles and flower arrangements and go home. I wanted nothing more to do with MS.

What was even more frustrating was the attitude I encountered from casual acquaintances who expressed doubt about my pain. When one woman insisted she knew many people with MS but had never heard of anyone who experienced pain with the disease, I was forced to defend myself against her skepticism. What do you say to such insensitivity? An actual demonstration of the sensation was an appealing notion and in keeping with my new pissy attitude.

Thank goodness Michael never put any constraints on my emotions or doubted for a moment the agony I was experiencing. In those first crazy-scary months he encouraged me to cry, even scream at the injustice of it all. I knew the question "why me?" was futile. Why *not* me? When thinking universally, it was entirely possible that I might draw the short straw. But we don't think universally, we think individually. On a personal basis, this was unfair and indicative of some huge cosmic error about which I was not pleased—to say the least. It was obvious that we needed some sort of strategy that didn't involve me whimpering pitifully or considering physical attacks on strangers.

Mercifully, when pain became a frequent obstacle to my enjoyment of the world, the act of cooking a meal could almost always mask the hurt for at least a little while. With my focus narrowed to the tiny confines of my kitchen, I edged away from the anguish into that safe, cozy world of bubbling sauces and warm, fragrant loaves of freshly baked bread. I could lose myself in the rhythmic, deliberate motions of my rolling pin on a long, slim slab of pasta dough. Consumed by measuring, sifting and kneading, I was transported to a state of intense concentration that left little room for pain. In my kitchen, I could hide from the tragedy my life was becoming.

Pain medication clearly wasn't the answer and I wasn't willing to become a useless pothead. As much as I enjoyed my kitchen, I certainly couldn't spend every minute there. It was time to find some means of creating joyfulness in my life.

Strolling through the dollar store, I had an idea. What's more uplifting than a theme party with lots of balloons and streamers? Valentine's Day provided the first opportunity for a little gaudy creativity.

## Menu:

*Homemade ricotta*
with freshly baked artisan bread

*Oysters on the half shell*

*Classic Caesar Salad*

*Grilled filet mignon*
over garlic mashed potatoes

*Sautéed spinach*
with crumbled blue cheese

*Flourless chocolate cake*
with raspberry sauce
and crème fraiche

## Guest list:

Steve & Molly
Jill & Ernie
Chip & Jeanne
Carly

"Our house looks like a gym on prom night," Michael grumbled.

"Beautiful, isn't it?"

Pushing aside the paper hearts I had artfully arranged on the table to spread out his newspaper, he grunted in response. You'd think an Italian would be more of a romantic.

"We're going to play a game tonight, and I need you to participate."

That announcement got his attention.

"You're kidding, right?"

"It will be fun. I promise. We're going to play *The Newlywed Game*, just like on television."

"We? You, maybe, but not me."

"How am I going to play without a partner?"

"Use Bella."

"Okay. Here's an idea. How about you act as the emcee for the night? You can be our Bob Eubanks and ask embarrassing, suggestive questions. You've always been good at that anyway."

With a sly grin, he went back to the newspaper.

A friend of mine had downloaded the original music from *The Newlywed Game* and sent it to me. I found actual questions from the TV show on the Internet and set up chairs to replicate the set. After dessert, we adjourned to our improvised soundstage and began the game. A sample of the questions: "If you could throw out one thing of your husband's, what would it be?" and "When will your wife say she was first kissed?" My personal favorite was "Which of your wife's friends would look best in a bikini?" because

Steve and Molly won the game when they named me, thereby producing an excessively hearty and incredulous laugh from my husband.

Jill and Ernie's daughter, Carly, had joined us for the evening because of love troubles. Carly's cad of a boyfriend had chosen the day before Valentine's Day to break up with her. During dinner Jeanne suggested each of us long-married couples relate to Carly how we had met and how to figure out if you've found the right mate. We also gave her a few tips about dating. Believe it or not, she took all of this very good-naturedly.

Fortunately, Carly is a professional chef and offered to lend me some much-needed assistance in the kitchen. Normally I stayed away from the wine before dinner was served so that I could keep my wits about me. But we had opened champagne, my downfall. I kept just sipping a little as I cooked, and before you knew it I was, well, a bit tipsy. I don't know how Julia Child did it. I heard she was snockered nearly every time she taped a show, dipping into the cooking sherry as she sautéed and flambéed. If I were to attempt that maneuver, a visit to the burn unit would follow.

Carly came to my rescue. She threw together a fabulous Caesar dressing for the salad and helped me grill the filets. Meanwhile I mashed the potatoes, a task that apparently can be done when you are smashed. Fortunately, I had made the dessert hours before and it was chilling in the fridge.

We had started dinner with the ricotta and bread. I had also asked Michael to reprise his skills from his job in college as an oyster-shucker and we served them on the half shell with our champagne. Apparently we hadn't invited many raw shellfish fans to this dinner, so I ate most of the oysters myself. Each one required a swig of champagne as a chaser, which started the whole fiasco in the kitchen.

In spite of the soused chef the meal was exquisite and during the game, we all laughed until we were weak.

Easter, Mother's Day, the Fourth of July and Halloween were all going to fall on a Sunday this year. What luck! But I wasn't about to wait for holidays to liven things up a bit. There were all sorts of party themes available.

We had a blast on Super Bowl Sunday, dressed in the jerseys of our favorite team, the Atlanta Falcons, and balancing plates on our laps as we watched the game. Not every meal had to be a sit-down, formal affair to count as an official Sunday gathering.

And Michael had already put in his request to reserve the entire table for his golf buddies on the Sunday of the Masters Tournament in April. He was a little concerned that my scurrying around setting the table, clanging pots in the kitchen and perhaps asking him to lift his feet so I could vacuum would cause him to miss a shot or two, but he was willing to risk it for a chance to get one of his favorite meals while watching hours of golf. For him and his pals I agreed to grill cheeseburgers, make homemade French fries and bake warm brownies for dessert. I did, however, decline his request that I don a maid's outfit for the evening.

The perfect night for a theme party was just a few weeks away, however. The Sunday of the Academy Awards is one of my favorite evenings of the year and I had an idea for a party that would match the glitz and glamour of the ceremony.

*March 7th – Gathering number ten*

*Menu:*

*Eleven assorted*

*appetizers*
to honor each
Oscar nominated movie

*Fresh popcorn*
with white truffle oil,
rosemary, sea salt and
shaved Asiago Cheese

*Guest list:*

Rob & Sabrina
Tom & Anita
Karin
Trish

Valuable lessons often result from painful experiences. Eleven appetizers? What was I thinking? I had decided making one dish to represent each nominated movie, along with some gourmet popcorn, would be a clever idea for our Sunday Oscar night party. It was the act of a lunatic. It didn't help that this year there was a record number of nominees. What ensued was hours of grilling, baking, frying and scurrying around in a frazzled frenzy.

I had "Pandora Spears," asparagus wrapped in phyllo dough, for *Avatar*. "Prawns Peri-Peri" represented *District 9*, and "Three Cheese Layovers" for *Up in The Air*. I even made mini hot dogs to honor the movie *Up*. There was fried chicken for *Precious*, sweet potato fries for *The Blind Side*, and mini bagels with crème cheese and lox for *A Serious Man*. Finally, I served a pine nut hummus with pita crackers for *The Hurt Locker*, English cheddar with biscuits for *An Education*, and pate with French bread for *Inglorious Basterds*. By the time I got the entire spread on the buffet table, I was as testy as an actress denied an Oscar for the tenth time in a row. Michael and his brother, Tommy, got their hands slapped more than once when they tried to dig into the food before all the others arrived.

I had asked all of our guests to come either in Oscar finery or as a character from one of the nominated movies. Everyone gamely accepted the challenge. Karin came as Jeff Bridges in *Crazy Heart*, although her costume had to be explained to the guests who had not yet seen the movie. We didn't want them leaping to the conclusion that she was showing up after a three week long bender. She tied Tommy for best dressed. He came as a sleazy film director, clutching his own self-awarded Oscar. Everyone filled out their ballots to vote for the winners and wine flowed.

After several glasses of chardonnay, I finally got past my exasperation over the fiasco that the menu had caused. It was yet one more great night in Sonoma.

## March 14th – Gathering number eleven

### Menu:

**Homemade ricotta**
with freshly baked artisan bread

**Field greens**
with balsamic vinaigrette

**Handmade ravioli**
with meat sauce

**Olive oil cake**
with homemade vanilla gelato

### Guest list:

Bill & Rose
Fred & Sandi
Tracy & Karen

After twelve weeks of dinner parties you would think I could reliably get the food to the table before the guests passed out from hunger. Apparently not. This week my problems weren't caused by a mouse, champagne or MS fatigue but an inability to grasp the concept of Daylight Saving Time.

I was sure I was on top of things. By noon I had my sauce bubbling along nicely. I had the bread rising. And the cake I had baked early in the morning was sitting on the counter, filling the house with a marvelous aroma. I had made two batches of ricotta, one for the appetizer and one for the ravioli. I even had the table set and all the napkins folded in these clever, origami-kind of shapes. All I had to do was roll out the ravioli dough and throw together the salad. But the sun was shining, and just back from a lovely walk with Bella, I didn't even look at the time. It couldn't possibly be even close to six o'clock with this much daylight left. Glancing at the clock I suddenly realized I had just a little over an hour in which to get the bread in the oven, make the dough for the ravioli, assemble said ravioli, whisk together ingredients for the vinaigrette and get dressed for the evening.

When our first guests arrived an hour early due to a similar inability to comprehend the whole time-change thing, I was scrambling around the kitchen with wet hair and no makeup.

The bread still needed another twenty minutes to bake when the rest of the crowd arrived. Michael started opening wine bottles, putting albums on the turntable and refilling everyone's glasses while keeping an eye on the chef. Somehow I had always managed to get the appetizers done on time. He looked worried. The little bowl of nuts was emptying fast. At last a very hot loaf of bread and a steaming lump of cheese appeared. Flavor: 9 points, Presentation: 0 points. They ate it anyway.

But ravioli with a very flavorful meat sauce, a Caesar salad and another loaf of bread made it to the table looking pretty darned good. Another dinner successfully, if a bit inelegantly, completed.

No one was more surprised than I was that the dinners kept making their way to the table week after week. The anticipation of yet another Sunday of friends and laughter was a powerful reason for putting forth the resistance necessary to override my pain and fatigue.

The fun didn't occur only on Sundays, though. On Monday mornings I was back in the kitchen for the cleanup. I never washed dishes on party night. It is an admittedly peculiar fetish, but a sink filled with warm, soapy water is a soul-soothing experience for me. As Martha-ish as it sounds, I actually like meticulously washing and drying each dish and fork and returning it to its rightful place in the cupboards.

I am a dish freak. Jewelry, fancy clothes, shoes… none of these purchases thrill me. But a store filled with hand-painted bowls and platters will have me whipping out the credit card for yet another acquisition. I have scores of dishes tucked into every available corner of my tiny house. Michael has been very tolerant of my obsession. When he went to Italy with his brother he ducked into every ceramic store he passed until he found a gorgeous matched hand-painted platter, bowl and pitcher that he thought I would love. He was right.

I often spent Tuesdays and Wednesdays poring over recipes and cookbooks. As do most passionate cooks, I view recipes as tools of inspiration, suggestions for tasty combinations rather than inflexible sets of instructions. I own a few cookbooks, but most of them sit idly on a shelf in my office. Michael Chiarello's is the only one allowed a place in my kitchen. I adore cooking magazines, though. I always quicken my steps back in to the house when my new *Cucina Italiana* magazine arrives in the mail. I love gazing at the photos of lavishly garnished dishes, photographed like runway models.

Some cooks taste everything. Some follow recipes to the letter. I cook with my sense of smell, and it hasn't failed me yet. I don't even use a timer when I bake. I know I have one on my stovetop, but I've never even tested it to see if it works. Friends and fellow cooks are incredulous when I tell them of my peculiar powers. How can you know if something is done if you don't hear a little bell ring? Perhaps that sense of smell that my grandmother lost in her youth was cosmically passed on to me in the form of a hyperawareness to aromas. From the back of the house, I can smell a cake that is minutes from perfection. With just a whiff of a sauce bubbling on the stove, I can tell it needs more seasoning. Michael used to doubt my abilities.

"How do I set the timer?" he yelled back to the bedroom on a day when fatigue had left me a limp mass in the middle of our bed.

"I haven't a clue." Bella, curled up beside me in dormant solidarity, looked up briefly. She didn't know either.

"How am I supposed to cook this then?" he whined.

I had purchased a supply of frozen meals for days like this. Long ago I had chased him from the kitchen, drawing an imaginary line across its entrance. I informed him early in our marriage that if he was hungry all he needed to do was make a request to his private chef. I never wanted to go back to the days when I was in a cooking competition with my spouse. The arrangement worked just fine for both of us. Michael was now permitted, however, to remove the cellophane from a frozen entrée and plop it in the oven whenever MS took me out of commission.

"I'll tell you when it's done."

"You'll watch the clock in there?"

"No. I'll just switch my nose into overdrive. I'll smell when it's ready."

"You're joking."

"I'm not and don't tell me how much time it says on the package either."

"Fine, but I'm going to take it out of the oven when you tell me to even if it is frozen in the middle or burnt to a crisp," he threatened.

"Now," I called out as soon as the scent of the perfectly cooked food wafted into my room.

"That's freaky. Exactly the amount of time the package suggested."

Of course. Grandma Mary would be proud.

On Thursday and Friday the thank-you cards would arrive in the mail. Either we have an exceedingly polite group of friends or the tradition of sending a nice, handwritten card to a hostess is alive and well in Sonoma. Either way, they were an enormous boost to my resolve. The beautiful cards and heartfelt gratitude expressed by our guests often moved me to tears. I have saved every one of them. I don't think people knew how important these dinners had become for me. Each week I was able to cook was crossed off the calendar as another victory. There was no way I was going to stop now.

Unfortunately, after several months of weekly dinner parties, Michael was losing his enthusiasm. In truth, neither of us had considered doing this for an entire year. We were certain that my health challenges, not to mention my resolve, would fail me. There is a trail of my ongoing projects residing in our garage—furniture I was going to restore, yards of fabric that might someday make it to the sewing machine, scrapbooks that were still just scraps; all were carefully stored in big plastic containers. My track record for hitting the finish line was not good.

Nor had either of us ever computed the financial impact of fifty-two dinner parties. I am not one to look at the price of food. If I need something for a recipe, I buy it. And if I'm going to put forth the effort to prepare a complicated dish, I'm going to purchase the best ingredients I can find. While I did attempt to use fresh, local ingredients and relatively economical cuts of meat, it was not an inexpensive endeavor to feed eight people every Sunday. Even with careful planning, most meals added up to at least one hundred dollars and that total didn't include the wine. Thankfully our guests were very generous, often showing up at our door with a bottle of wine in each hand. Many were winery owners or involved in the industry in some fashion. Our table was often graced with numerous bottles of excellent vintages.

Even the most humble Sonoma abode is likely to house a treasure trove of wine. I once visited the home of an elderly couple who invited me over to view their extensive book collection and, as is proper etiquette in wine country, they offered me a glass of wine. I was surprised when they then escorted me downstairs to their wine cellar. It is the rare home in California that sports a basement. Theirs housed an enormous collection of wines that encompassed the entire subsection of their Queen Anne Victorian. No one would have guessed that these two eighty-year-olds had several thousand bottles of wine stored beneath their modest home. No matter how long they lived they would never manage to drink it all. I let them refill my glass.

The bounty of Sonoma could make Bacchus blush. We are surrounded by vineyards, wineries and wine-makers. Every event that occurs in this town involves wine in some fashion. They even serve it at funerals. The local movie theater offers wine. The corner coffee house pours it by the glass. Every book club, charity organization and rotary meeting is expected to provide a little wine for its members. This is a very congenial town.

With Michael working as the publisher of the premier wine country visitor publication, we were especially in tune with the wine industry. Every month our calendar had at least one or two wine events scheduled. On any given weekend several wineries offered a barrel tasting, hosted a wine pairing, or threw a party. It would be tough to be a teetotaler in this place. Obviously, that wasn't a problem for Michael and me. We embraced the culture with glass in hand.

Best of all, there is a marvelous tradition of mutual price reductions for those in the business. It is called the "inter-winery discount." Each winery offers to its brethren in the field a break on the price of its wines, usually around thirty percent. Many families try to arrange for one member to work at least part-time at a tasting room to garner this markdown. Even if your wine cellar is a modest hall closet, you at least have the opportunity to keep it well stocked.

Michael always acted as sommelier for our gatherings, selecting wines to pair with each course of the meal. Prior to my illness, he had briefly considered leaving the publishing field to take a job in the wine industry. Over the years, he had attended numerous classes in wine appreciation and winemaking techniques. To say that he landed a dream job as the publisher of *Wine Country This Week* was an understatement. It was the perfect opportunity for Michael to indulge in his passion for wine, while contributing his wealth of experience to a magazine he loved.

Nearly everyone attending our Sunday dinners brought along a bottle of wine, so we had to pull only a couple from our own racks. By our calculations, however, my little challenge was still going to add up to something in the neighborhood of five thousand dollars by the year's end. That amount was almost exactly what we usually budgeted for an annual vacation. I also hadn't taken into account that the obligation to be home every Sunday would make it impossible to squeeze in any extended time away. Michael wasn't sure he was willing to forego a vacation and set aside the bulk of our entertainment budget for Sunday dinners. I didn't blame him for grousing about relinquishing the opportunity for a break from his job. He was the sole breadwinner in our home as well as my emergency room attendant and chief hand-holder. He certainly deserved a vacation.

But this project of mine had become my own private Mount Everest. It was the ultimate test of my resolve and my means of holding on to as much normalcy as I could. I still had plenty of climbing ahead, but I clearly could not stop now. If ever there was something in my life I needed to see through to the end, this was it. I could donate those unfinished quilts, take the old furniture to Goodwill and toss out the scrapbook junk, but this was the one undertaking I could not abandon. Quitting this challenge wouldn't be just another instance of procrastination or my well-known propensity for being a bit flaky. It would mean that MS had won. I may not be good at staying the course, but I am a competitor and I don't like to lose.

When we sat down and I explained my feelings to him, Michael did an about-face. He became my champion and my head cheerleader. He promised that if I faltered, he would carry me to the finish line. Together we were going to make this happen. Even the financial issue took on a different tenor. As Michael put it, "We're deciding to put our money in friendships this year."

It turned out to be the best investment we ever made.

*I wish I was a glow worm,*
*A glow worm's never glum*
*'Cos how can you be grumpy*
*When the sun shines out your bum?*

**~Author Unknown**

## *three*

Wouldn't it be crazy if after all the years of research scientists discovered that, in fact, laughter is the best medicine? It certainly was keeping me going. While wine fueled the frivolity, the warm spring and summer nights of Sonoma and the shared bounty of the meal were a wonderful impetus for merriment. On many nights, we simply laughed ourselves silly.

## Menu:

### Homemade pizza
with four cheeses

### Field greens
with balsamic vinaigrette

### Grill whole salmon
with wilted mint & basil
and grilled lemons

### Assorted grilled
### spring vegetables
### Olive oil cake
with homemade pistachio gelato

## Guest list:

Paul & MaryBeth
Mary & Gerry
Chris
Mary F.

My friend Mary had accepted our invitation and was bringing along her husband Gerry. During a conversation a day or two earlier she let it slip that Gerry had a rather unique occupation in his past. He was Bozo the Clown! I was totally blown away. This icon of my youth was coming to my home for dinner. I called my brother in New Zealand just to tell him and he dropped the phone. Another clue that we had a somewhat odd childhood, I guess.

We found Gerry to be a lovely, gracious man but not the big, goofy clown from my memory. He laughed with us and told some stories, but it wasn't until we asked him to "do" Bozo that he transformed. It was fantastic. All of a sudden we knew, beyond a shadow of doubt, that he was truly the real Bozo.

Most folks at the tennis courts in Sonoma would never guess that Gerry, an eighty-one-year-old with the zest and stamina of a teenager, had been a star with a name so famous that every kid in America knew him.

Gerry related how he used to travel from one gig to another with a magician in tow. The magician was always at the wheel because the enormous wig and size 32 shoes made driving impossible for Bozo the Clown. He got a great laugh out of us when he did an impression of the looks the two got as they navigated the streets of San Francisco.

He said his greatest joy, however, came from visiting hospitals to entice smiles from ailing children.

With the exception of Bozo the Clown, none of our friends was a professional funny person, but with jokes, silly games, and side-splitting stories, each had us falling off our chairs with laughter. Our tiny backyard is ringed by the backyards of adjacent homes, and I'm quite certain that our uproarious outbursts could be heard by each of our very tolerant and good-natured neighbors. We avoided most complaints by putting nearly every one of them on our guest list, but there were some people on the block whom I had not met. One day I attempted to make amends by walking around and introducing myself to the folks who had the misfortune of sharing a back fence with such boisterous neighbors.

I discovered that the woman who resided directly behind us was living with a severely disabled young girl for whom she provided care. I apologized for our loud parties and asked her if the two of them would like to join us. She declined my offer but told me that the sounds of joy and laughter emanating from our yard every Sunday night provided them with the highlight of their week. On warm, summer nights, she would wheel her young friend out to their backyard to listen to the sounds of the party. Simply hearing others enjoying themselves was enough to brighten their lives. I walked away with an even firmer resolve to keep the joyfulness flowing…and to give Gerry a call. His services were needed again.

## Menu:

### Pizza
with Yukon gold potatoes,
rosemary & gorgonzola

### Handmade ravioli
with fresh tomato and basil
sauce & grilled Italian sausages

### Field greens
with pears and sliced almonds

### Orange almond cake
with rum raisin gelato

### Guest list:

Dave & Rebecca
Mike & Phyllis
Susan & Alan
Scott

Sunday morning arrived, the sun was shining and the sky was crystal blue. With temperatures in the eighties it was the perfect day for an outdoor dinner party. Our little backyard was all spruced up and I had just finished sewing a new tablecloth with matching cushions for the chairs. Everything was shipshape except the hostess. Fatigue had hit me hard. I wrote my to-do list in the morning and then just sat and stared at it. I was wading through the mud again. I had food to buy and a table to set. I needed to clean the bathrooms, vacuum, sweep the back patio and give the dog a bath. And then, with all the energy and enthusiasm that remained, I would prepare a four-course meal for eight people entirely from scratch. I didn't need a to-do list. I needed a good psychiatrist.

As I slogged through the aisles of the grocery store, lifting cartons of milk that felt as heavy as stone, I had to fight the urge to just plop down next to the canned tomatoes in a semi-catatonic heap.

When I finally reached home I slumped into the couch before tackling item number two on the list: make the gelato. It was a simple custard gelato. Unfortunately brain-fog, another charming MS symptom, had crept up on me. Not once, but twice, I cooked the custard too fast and caused it to fail. The broken shells of a dozen wasted eggs filled the sink. With my resolve fading fast, I began mentally listing all the restaurants in town that delivered.

Michael came to my rescue, leading me to a comfy chaise lounge in a shady corner of the backyard and tackling all of the housekeeping chores. While I rested he even headed off to the store for more eggs.

Back in my kitchen after a nice nap, I took on the gelato one more time. Mercifully, batch number three succeeded. I added cinnamon, rum-soaked raisins and chopped pecans to the custard and it tasted sublime. Nothing gets me going like a dish that comes together perfectly. I took on the almond orange cake next and produced a golden, aromatic piece of heaven that caused the entire house to smell like a swanky French bakery. Now I was cooking! Next I rolled out the pizza dough, prepared the ravioli filling and completed the prep work for the pizza. I had decided to try a new combination of ingredients this week. After spreading olive oil on the dough, I added Yukon gold potatoes, gorgonzola and rosemary. A scattering of caramelized onions completed the pie. With the ravioli bobbing in the pasta pot and the sausages sizzling on the grill, I whipped up the salad and cut up tomatoes, basil and garlic for the fresh tomato sauce.

Nothing more needed to be done. All the food had been served and I was curled into a cozy chair under a warm, star-lit sky. I looked around at a crowd of smiling friends, savoring the last bites of their meal, engaged in animated conversations and enjoying magnificent wine. It dawned on me that I no longer felt the weight of MS. Once again the magic worked.

But how long could I count on pasta and friends to heal me?

A healthy dose of fear can be a good thing. It can warn you away from dangerous situations, producing a life-saving fight-or-flight response. But fear can also paralyze you. Each time a flare-up occurred, I feared the worst. If the lesion on my spine became active again I might lose the ability to walk. If the lesion on my optic nerve acted up I could be permanently blind. And it would happen overnight. No forewarning, no time for preparation.

While I certainly didn't expect life in a wheelchair to be a picnic, the thought of life without sight was terrifying. I might not be able to control my unruly immune system, but I could rein in my panic. The first task at hand was simply to dismiss the notion of blindness. No amount of emotional prep-work would prepare me for that anyway. So I put it out into the universe: I'll accept nearly anything else, but please let me keep my eyesight.

Getting a handle on fear was next on the agenda. I had become like Redd Foxx in the old television series *Sanford and Son*. At the first sign of a flare-up, I would figuratively clutch my chest and declare, "It's the big one!"

But I soon realized that letting go of the panic I felt each time I became symptomatic was a crucial component to living with MS. Whenever a bout of pain, fatigue or tremors occurred and then faded away again I got better at not overreacting. I knew the "big one" was around the corner somewhere, but it wasn't here now.

Living in the moment is an acquired skill, but the reward is that you begin to realize that a warm afternoon spent basking in the sun, a stroll by the creek with your loyal dog, or the taste of a sweet, ripe strawberry is cause for celebration. The diagnosis of a serious medical condition can cause you to snap to attention. The trick is to pay attention to the right things.

Gradually, I was learning to accept this new body of mine and realized that even though it was misbehaving in some ways, it was also bringing me much greater awareness of what was important in life. It would be absurd to conclude that the disease was a piece of good fortune, however. In reality, it was more like a term that Michael's ex-wife had created. She dubbed such situations as a "blurse"…both a blessing and a curse. I hadn't realized I needed a wake-up call, and this was certainly not one I would have ordered for myself, but the truth was clear. Multiple Sclerosis had proven to be a valuable means of increasing my appreciation for those marvelous little moments in life that I had been letting go unnoticed. On good days, I could actually conjure up a little gratitude for the blurse that life had handed me.

The thoughtfulness of our many friends was also a source of mental healing. However, in an effort to be helpful, some people crossed the line into an area I called "The Cure Conversation." It was a subject I always dreaded. An astute friend, who also happens to be a physician, once observed that "there's an expert on every barstool."

Chanting numerical sequences, the daily reciting of inspirational sayings (You can decide to be well! It is all in your power!), "a very special MS cure" offered by a friend's chiropractor, a vial of holy water from Lourdes, and an exceptionally nasty suggestion of vitamin enemas were all offered as surefire therapies guaranteed to end my suffering. When I respectfully declined these treatments, I was viewed with suspicion. Didn't I want to get better?

My standard reply to any offer of information about a miracle cure was to encourage the one who discovered the amazing remedy to contact the National MS Society. I told concerned friends and acquaintances that tens of thousands of people were suffering much more than I, and if they indeed knew of a cure for MS, then their information needed to reach this wonderful organization. I highly doubt anyone ever contacted them.

These people were eager to be helpful. They meant no harm. But as anyone who has faced a serious medical issue discovers, miracle cures abound in the universe and woe to the patient who refuses to explore these options. I was accused of being closed-minded, of buying into a conspiracy on the part of the traditional medical community to keep me ill and - the one that really got my blood boiling - of secretly enjoying the attention I was receiving from being sick. I wanted to slap the woman who said that.

More fervently than anyone could know, I wanted a cure. I wanted to watch my grandson grow up. I wanted to be a healthy, vibrant partner to my husband in his retirement years, capable of exploring the world with him. I didn't want any more pain. I wanted my old life back.

But as Michael told me, in his years of searching for a cure for his ailing mother, he found no miracle. Just wanting something with all your heart won't make it happen, and heeding the call of snake-oil salesmen has rarely proven to be a wise route to health. Not that I had my head in the sand. I was constantly searching the Internet for news of promising drug trials. However, I was well aware that this disease has been studied extensively by a wide array of scientists, and an outright cure has been elusive. It could happen, but chances are that it won't come in time to help me. Even an upbeat attitude can't change that.

I had already endured over a year of daily, self-inflicted injections of a medication that was supposed to ward off future attacks. The painful shots left me with welts and bruises. I became a human pin cushion in an effort to stay well. When I could not face that needle one more time, I opted to hold off and wait for a better treatment choice. Surely the pharmaceutical industry would come up with a more humane method for dealing with MS.

My friend Jeanne was not in a position to be quite as cavalier about drug therapy. She was declining rapidly and desperately needed a treatment that worked. She had recently been accepted into a new drug trial that offered the possibility of regaining some of her mobility and halting the progression of her MS. Unfortunately, as summer drew to a close it became apparent either she had received the placebo in the blind test or the drug had been just another in a long line of dead ends. In the course of a year, we watched the struggle to make her legs move become increasingly difficult. Her days using a walker for even short distances were coming to a close. To help her enter our home now, we had to lift her feet and hoist her up each step to the door.

Jeanne and I had been introduced through a mutual friend who knew of my diagnosis. Michael and I had just moved to Sonoma and our friend thought meeting someone who was afflicted with the same disease might be helpful for me. MS proved to be one of the least significant things we had in common. Jeanne shares my love of people. With her easy smile and straightforward approach, she is the type of person who does not invite drama into her world, particularly around her disability. The message she conveys is "Pay no attention to this walker. It is of no importance and it is definitely not who I am." Life is too short to wallow in tribulations. Jeanne is all about having fun. In short, she was the perfect friend to help me keep my head on straight.

Most people don't know how to deal with someone who is battling a challenging disease. There seems to be several distinct responses. For me, the exceedingly sympathetic tactic was particularly grating. People meant it kindly, but when a pained expression crossed their face and they patted my hand instead of shaking it, I knew what would follow. They would start with an overly cheery greeting such as, "I am *so* pleased to meet you," and then slide into excessively praising my courage. The act of acquiring a disease did not automatically make me someone to be admired, nor did it make me courageous.

Equally annoying are people who try to commiserate by listing their minor ailments. I once met a woman who began our conversation with "I know just how you feel" and then went on to give me a long-winded description of her battle with foot fungus. But the deniers are the most galling of all. Their confident, upbeat proclamations that are supposedly meant to cheer you often leave you feeling as though you need to defend the severity of your diagnosis. It is hard to know what to say when someone spouts, "I hear they are close to a cure. You're going to have this all behind you in no time," or "You look great! I bet you don't even have MS." There are no responses to these declarations that don't sound whiny or pessimistic. A tight smile and a terse "I hope you're right" is the only rejoinder that is likely to end the sanguinity.

The best reaction I ever got, however, came at a cocktail party soon after I was diagnosed. I was using a cane, and a young man approached me and asked if I had hurt my leg. I explained that I had just been diagnosed with Multiple Sclerosis. He looked me in the eye and simply said, "That sucks." We both laughed at his succinct, honest reply. Then we segued into a lively political exchange that was much more interesting than a discussion of my disease.

Jeanne was a veteran of the disability game, yet I never saw a single crack in her emotional armor until one day when I was helping her into her car. After navigating my front porch step, we began the process of loading her walker into the car and hoisting her into the driver's seat. As we struggled together to get her situated behind the wheel of her specially equipped van, our eyes met.

Her voice cracked as she said to me, "I hope you don't ever get this bad."

"I hope not too," was the only way to respond.

Fortunately, by the end of the year, Jeanne's doctors had suggested a new drug therapy designed to help MS patients walk better. It worked. Her army of friends got to enjoy the sight of her navigating steps with increasing strength and confidence. Maybe there were a few miracles to be had after all.

# May 9th (Mother's Day) – Gathering number nineteen

## Menu:

### Assorted cheeses,
olive and rosemary almonds

### Traditional lasagna
with Italian sausage and beef short ribs

### Field greens
with balsamic vinaigrette

### Mandarin orange cake
with coconut frosting

## Guest list:

Sophie & Luc
Mark & Michelle
Chris & Alicia

Our youngest guests of the year were the five-year-old twins from next door. For their very first dinner party they got all dressed up and tried their best to display proper manners. They were actually better behaved than a few of the adults we had hosted.

I went rather simple with the menu knowing my young guests would not like their food too fancy. I started a nice sauce for lasagna on the stove early in the morning. All day our house was filled with the aroma of a bubbling brew of tomatoes, short ribs, Italian sausage and spices. I baked a very pretty mandarin orange cake with a coconut frosting, but purchased ice cream to go with it. I had planned to make a pizza, but with the drizzle that awaited me at the outdoor grill, I wasn't at all disappointed when my pizza dough failed to rise. I'm not sure what happened, perhaps bad yeast. On other Sundays this turn of events might have caused angst. but this Sunday I was in no mood for drama. It was Mother's Day. A nice platter of cheese, olives and nuts would do just fine.

Around four o'clock I began assembling the lasagna, tossing the salad and putting the finishing touch on the cake with an arrangement of lemon leaves and blossoms. This dinner was so easy, so relaxed, I even had time to spruce up a bit before the guests arrived. I actually had clean clothes on when everyone came to the door. As they entered, everyone received a glass of champagne or sparkling cider and we made a toast to the mothers. The champagne helped me get over a snit-fit that had been brewing all day. No cards, no flowers had arrived from the four boys. Only Bella remembered me with a lovely gift certificate to enjoy a day at the spa, cementing her position as my favorite child.

Of the many joys we discovered about our new home none was more entertaining than the twins. Sophie and Luc brought back so many memories of life with small children. If they heard us in our backyard they'd peer through the fence and talk to us in their sweet, lisp-filled voices. Michael had them squealing with delight whenever he threatened "noogies," his form of child torture involving a hearty head scrubbing.

A perfect summer day was one in which the air was filled with their high-pitched giggles as they set up their Slip 'n Slide on our front lawn. They are simply delightful. It seems as we've age, we've moved further and further away from a life that includes kids. Even grandchildren are only a temporary distraction from our mature lifestyle. Having Sophie and Luc around was a wonderful way to enjoy that youthful energy and spirit again. Why would anyone want to live in a retirement community?

Like so many others, parents Michelle and Marc struggled a bit starting a family. Fortunately, they were eventually able to welcome a matched set of son and daughter with star-caliber cuteness. Luc is full of big grins and grand ideas. He has the demeanor of an eight-week-old Labrador puppy, bouncing around his father's legs as they go on walks together. Sophie is a blond fairy princess who refuses to wear anything but frilly dresses. She is so sweet that when I was experiencing a tough day with MS, she came over with her favorite teddy bear to act, on loan, as a soothing companion.

They were like a couple of kids sent by central casting and they were the most polite children we had ever met, not surprising considering I never once heard their mother raise her voice. Whatever happened to screeching like a fishwife as a parenting technique? My two rowdy boys could transform me into a sharp-tongued shrew in a matter of minutes. But Michelle never went off script. I'm going to come back as one of her children when I die.

We soon learned that our little neighborhood wasn't done growing. Our neighbors to the left, Chris and Alicia, announced at one of our gatherings that they were expecting their first child, a little girl, by the end of the year. We were thrilled. Alicia is a social worker for a hospice organization. She has an air of calmness and wisdom that most people don't obtain until late in life, if ever. She was unfazed by the chaos that was about to enter their lives. Michelle and I both rolled our eyes when she showed us her nursery just a few weeks before the baby was due. Nothing was in order. We both gasped when Alicia breezily told us she was sure a baby wouldn't need much. Months before my first son's arrival I had outfitted my house like I was expecting an army of babies.

Sure enough, when Emma Rose arrived near the end of the year Chris and Alicia wove her seamlessly into the fabric of their lives. With her shocking mass of dark brown hair and cupid lips she charmed the entire block, but none more than Michael and me, the newly appointed neighborhood grandparents.

# Menu:

## Pizza
with Yukon gold potatoes,
rosemary & gorgonzola

## Grilled chicken
with assorted grilled
summer vegetables

## Grilled cornbread,
## arugula and tomato
## salad

## Strawberry tiramisu
with homemade ginger gelato

## Guest list:

Dan & Tessa

Peter

Marybeth

Kit & Jerry

All day long I watched the sky. Was it going to get sunny? Was the wind coming up? By the time our guests arrived, the idea of al fresco dining seemed ridiculous, but I have never been one to face facts. The drapes were whipping around the patio, the wine was chilling nicely with no need for refrigeration and still I stood, wrapped in a sweater, barbeque tongs in hand. If I willed it so, maybe a little global warming would occur in my backyard.

Tessa, my old friend from the days of our radio show *Book Talk*, had driven up from Albany with her husband Dan, and his brother Peter. I wanted everything to be perfect. I had made a lovely strawberry tiramisu the day before. I also bought this fancy-schmancy air-chilled, organic chicken for about the same price as filet mignon and it had been marinating for the past twenty-four hours.

Dan and Tessa are serious "foodies" as well as accomplished writers. They were bringing with them a couple of new friends, Jerry and his wife Kit. Jerry used to write for the *National Enquirer*. They, too, were culinary experts. The pressure was on. And of course nearly everything that could go wrong did.

The weather had me in a tizzy, but my decision to grill nearly every dish also caused a problem. Thank goodness Michael had the foresight to run out to the hardware store an hour before the guests arrived to buy an extra canister of propane. Halfway through grilling the chicken breasts, I found them lying limp and uncooked on a cold grill. Michael swooped in, changed the tank, and saved the day.

The grill had seen a lot of action by then. My salad recipe called for grilled cornbread. You bake the cornbread in the oven, cool it and then cut it into inch-thick strips. I was supposed to then brush each strip with olive oil and place them on the grill for a minute or two until slightly toasted. Sound simple? Have you ever tried to pick up a piece of cornbread with barbeque tongs? The damn stuff just crumbled, fell through the grill and promptly caught on fire.

I had two pizzas on the menu, as well. Pizzas are my specialty. I've made scores of them over the last few years. I went to Italy to learn how to make pizzas. This part of the meal should have been a no-brainer, but once again, my dough failed to rise. What the heck was happening? When a second batch was also looking decidedly flat after an hour, I called my son and fellow pizza expert, Dan, for some advice. He told me to try putting it in a warm oven and covering it with a damp dishcloth. It worked. By the time the guests arrived, I had the first of two pizzas sizzling nicely on the grill. A potato, gorgonzola, and pancetta pie got rave reviews. Next I experimented with a new pizza: smoked salmon, red onion, capers, and gruyere. I had no opportunity to taste it but Tessa gave me a "thumbs up."

At least the pizzas were holding up my reputation as a good cook with the crowd of culinary connoisseurs at the table.

In the last ten years or so, there has emerged a fanatical element in the ranks of those of us who enjoy making pizzas. Not that I fault anyone for building a wood-burning brick pizza oven in their backyard. I'd do it myself if I had the room and a lot of extra money lying around. But when you can no longer imagine eating a pizza that wasn't made with "000" flour flown in from Italy, you may have gone too far.

I first fell in love with real pizzas when I went to Naples. They are nothing like the calorie-laden, gooey messes that most Americans think of as pizza. The crust is thin but not crispy or cracker-like. The toppings are very sparse, just a sprinkling of cheese and a few bits of vegetables or meat. One person, even a light eater, can easily consume an entire pie. The proper way to eat one is to fold it twice, creating a multi-layered "slice." The ingredients are fresh, the flavors pure and simple…the essence of Italian cooking.

I returned from cooking school in Italy armed with the recipe for great dough and the inspiration to try some innovative pizzas for my family and friends. I couldn't build a pizza oven, but I could do the next best thing. I bought a high-quality pizza stone and a large wooden paddle. I was in business.

Making pizza is an art. No two pies are the same, and even if you use the same recipe, the same methods and the same equipment, you're still going to get variations. Yeast is a fussy little organism.

The recipe is deceptively simple. You just add a half tablespoon of dry yeast to a half cup of warm water and then pour it into a bowl with two cups of a high-quality baking flour, a generous teaspoon of sea salt, a tablespoon of olive oil and one-third cup of milk. I also like to throw in a little chopped fresh rosemary. Stir it thoroughly and throw a warm towel over the bowl. Let it rise for at least three hours; overnight is better.

It's what you do to the dough after it rises that separates the amateurs from the pros. The best method for achieving a perfect crust is to toss the dough in the air, allowing the spinning motion to create the ideal size and thickness. For the life of me, however, I cannot throw a pizza. My son Dan has attempted to teach me numerous times, but I have always been inept at tossing dough in the air and catching it. The fact that countless acne-prone teenagers, at seven dollars an hour, flawlessly execute this maneuver in pizzerias across the country only added to my frustration. After dropping more than one pizza, I simply gave up and dug out my wooden rolling pin. I could hear the collective gasps of aficionados every time I mistreated my pizza dough by rolling it like a cheap piecrust. Sometimes you have to own your deficiencies.

But what I lacked in dough tossing I made up for in creativity. Each week I experimented with pizza toppings that were innovative, even bordering on brazen. My pear, caramelized onion and pecan pizza was heavenly. A smoked salmon with shaved red onion and feta was equally well-received. Yukon gold potatoes, sliced as thin as paper, are delectable on a pizza when paired with gorgonzola cheese and pancetta. When the figs began ripening on the trees in the neighborhood, I obtained permission to gather all I needed for my Sunday dinners. A pizza with figs, goat cheese and fresh rosemary is culinary poetry.

I couldn't wait to tell my cooking teacher in Italy about my discoveries. When I returned for a second go-around at the cooking school in Sorrento I cornered Carmen and told her how I had produced some lively new adaptations of her recipes. When she heard my list of ingredients she icily announced, "In Italy we would shoot you for that."

Oh well, we Americans have never been good at following rules.

*May 23rd – Gathering number twenty-one*

## Menu:

**Pizza**
with smoked salmon, red onion and feta cheese

*Classic Caesar salad*

*Old-fashioned spaghetti and meatballs*

*Chocolate gratine*
with orange gelato

## Guest list:

Bob & Barbara
Jean & Doug
Zanne & Macon

For many years my culinary "holy grail" has been a perfect meatball, one that rivals those Michael's Sicilian grandmother used to make. It must be moist, tender and full of flavor, reminding him of the Sunday dinners of his youth when all of his relatives gathered around to eat pasta, drink wine and yell at each other.

Once again, I attempted to achieve a meatball that would bring my husband to tears. I combined freshly ground lamb and beef and added fresh-picked spices, gently sautéed onions and garlic, homemade bread-crumbs soaked in beer (a tip from an Italian friend of mine) and grated parmesan cheese. I then formed the mixture into large meatballs and browned them in olive oil and placed them in the oven to bake for thirty minutes. When first sampled, right from the oven, they tasted wonderful. However, by the time they made it to the table several hours later, despite being slathered in marinara sauce, they had hardened into nearly inedible, tasteless brown lumps that would have made excellent bocce balls.

Each of our very polite and forgiving guests offered sympathy and kind remarks. "With lots of sauce, they're not too bad" was one line I heard several times. I noticed, however, that no one reached for a second helping.

I have attempted dozens of recipes trying to find one reminiscent of the meatballs of Michael's youth. With every combination of ingredients, the results just seemed to get worse. The hard, tasteless wads of meat could have been driven two hundred yards down a fairway. How could it be so difficult to make a tender, succulent meatball? Fortunately, before Michael put his foot down and refused to eat one more of my failed experiments, my friend Sue came to my rescue with her Grandma Petrello's recipe.

To make a magnificent meatball it seems you have to start with ground veal. I'm as squeamish as the next person about eating a baby cow, but I had become so frustrated by my inability to create an edible meatball that I was willing to compromise my ethics.

To make Grandma Petrello's meatballs, start with three pounds of veal, a cup and a half of plain breadcrumbs, two-thirds cup of grated Romano cheese, four eggs and two egg whites. To this mixture add a quarter cup of chopped fresh basil, six cloves of minced garlic and a tablespoon of salt. Using your hands, gently work all of the ingredients together and form about two dozen large meatballs, then roll them in a little more of the breadcrumbs and brown them for a few minutes in a hot skillet with two or three tablespoons of olive oil. Finish cooking them in a hearty sauce for at least two hours.

When I placed one of these succulent morsels in front of Michael and he took his first bite, I knew I finally had gotten it right. The blissful look on his face said it all.

If you want an Italian man to fall in love with you, serve him a good meatball.

## Menu:

### Pizzas:

Yukon gold potatoes, rosemary
and gorgonzola

Classic margarita

Fig and goat cheese with
caramelized onion

Italian sausage
with grilled summer vegetables

### Salad of field greens

with rosemary pecans
and balsamic vinaigrette

### Fresh picked
### strawberries over shortcake

with homemade strawberry
ice cream

### Guest list:

Sue M.
Barbara
Sue Y.
Jane
Michelle
Alicia
Karen

Michael was going to be spending the entire next week in Southern California for business, and not even good meatballs could keep him home. He would stay the weekend in San Diego with his buddies to enjoy some much needed golf and sailing time. But, by day two of his absence, I was really missing him. When he called home, however, I kept quiet about the pain, fatigue and loneliness I was experiencing. He deserved a break.

Since the day I was diagnosed, he had been by my side. I had never had to grapple with this disease on my own before. For an entire week I had no one to bring me a sandwich when I was too fatigued to get off the couch. I had no one to hold me in the night when pain made sleep impossible. I had no one to make me laugh when I wanted to just sit down and cry. For the first time, I faced the realization of how frightening and difficult it would be to travel this road alone.

What I needed was a good dose of girl-friends. Pharmaceutical companies have tried, but they've never discovered a drug that can compete with the power of best friends. Michael's absence presented the perfect opportunity to throw a party for my women friends. Best of all, Kathy could finally attend one of my dinners. I sent out the message to all the women on my list and waited for the replies. They came in droves. I received e-mails from a host of wonderful friends, all anxious to get in on the fun. But the one I needed most never arrived. Kathy wasn't coming. I didn't call and ask why. I didn't want to hear her struggle for an excuse.

Encouraging our guests to tell their stories was a key element of our gatherings. Each week we tried to set a mood that allowed people to feel comfortable sharing the details about the events and people who had shaped their lives. Women seldom need prompting to talk, but I had an idea for a new tactic to jumpstart the conversations.

I asked each of my girlfriends to bring a photograph of themselves as a teenager. We passed them around, laughing at our old hairstyles and marveling at our youthful figures. Then I posed the question, "What would that girl think of the woman she became?" We each mused silently for a few minutes, thinking back to what our hopes had been and trying to remember where we had expected life to take us. We stared at the faces of our younger selves and wondered, "Would she be proud of me?"

The stories that emerged were touching, funny and sometimes heartbreaking. Even the younger women at the table, Michelle and Alicia, had moving tales to tell. Both were in their thirties so it wasn't difficult for them to remember the ambitions they had as teenagers.

Karen, another guest, is an attractive, vibrant woman who makes her living as a school administrator. She is well-respected by her peers and loved by her students, and I've known her for nearly two decades. Yet when it came time for her to share her thoughts, she had to take a moment to compose herself. She had not brought a photograph, and we soon learned the painful reason.

"I destroyed most of the photos of myself from that time."

To our amazement, we learned that our confident, outgoing friend had not always been so. She told us that she had been overweight in her teens and as a result was a lonely and miserable young woman, but she also had harbored a secret during those years.

"In spite of my weight what I really wanted to be was an actress," she confessed. "I just knew I'd be laughed at if I ever tried to get on a stage, though. It was an extremely painful chapter in my life."

With time she lost the weight but not the dream. There wasn't a dry eye at the table when she announced that she had joined a community theater troupe and was about to finally enjoy the sound of applause.

"My teenage self would have never imagined her life could be so wonderful," Karen said. "I just wish I could reach back and tell her about all the fabulous things that were ahead of her."

A few months later another friend and I went to her opening night. She was in the play *Gypsy!* as, of all things, a stripper. We clapped louder than everyone else in the theater.

*The* place where optimism most
flourishes is the lunatic asylum.

**~Havelock Ellis**

*four*

It was to be the most memorable gathering in my year-long commitment to sharing our table. Five of the men I love most in this world would be together for the first time. Michael, my two sons, my brother who had traveled all the way from New Zealand to be a part of my fifty-two dinners, and the newest member of this elite group, my grandson Jackson – Only my beloved stepsons, Nick and Tony, would be unable to make it. I was overwhelmed by the sight of them laughing with one another and enjoying each other's company, and it dawned on me that to love and be loved by such amazing guys was probably the greatest blessing of my life.

Past generations lived closer to their relatives than most families do today. In those days it was seldom a problem to fill the chairs at a family dinner on a Sunday evening. But like most modern families, we have rarely been able to gather the clan together. With family members scattered hundreds of miles apart we were lucky to get even a few of them to the table for one of our gatherings. Sometimes we wondered why we felt the need to make the effort. But families are like fudge, sweet and wonderful, with just a couple of nuts thrown in to liven things up.

## June 27th – Gathering number twenty-six

## Menu:

### Pizza
with wild mushrooms and
Italian sausage

### Grilled tri-tip

### Watermelon and mint salad

### Corn on the cob
with queso fresco and lime

### Strawberry shortcake
with crème fraiche

### Guest list:

Dan & Abbie
Patrick & Amanda
My grandson, Jackson
My brother, Bill

My oldest son Dan is married to a lovely girl from Hong Kong. Abbie and he met on a cruise to Mexico when Dan, a teacher, was chaperoning a senior class trip and Abbie was vacationing with her mother. It was love at first sight. After meeting the rest of the family, this charming young woman actually agreed to join our crazy clan and they were married on a sun-lit day in the rose gardens of Portland, Oregon.

They now live in a remote section of the Northern California coastline. Their little town of Shelter Cove is home to eight hundred ascetic souls who have denied themselves fancy restaurants, movie theaters and even a decent grocery store in favor of soaring cliffs, gigantic redwoods and a nearly deserted black sand beach. Dan teaches in one of the smallest schools in the entire state. From kindergarten to the twelfth grade the entire student body consists of only forty-two children. The main industries in the area are sports fishing and marijuana growing, which makes for a rather eclectic cast of characters at PTA meetings. Somehow the rednecks, aging hippies and reclusive retirees co-exist in relative harmony. My petite daughter-in-law represents just about the only example of ethnic diversity in the area. However, if they thought this sweet, little Chinese girl was all shy smiles and genteel manners, they were soon to realize otherwise. The Annual Southern Humboldt County Cook-off inspires scores of competitors to vie for the coveted prize of Best Barbeque. After only her second year of competition, Abbie managed to deliver a thrashing to the reigning chefs of the area, taking home the top prize with her magnificent barbequed pineapple ribs.

Cooking was a skill handed down for generations in her family. When I first got home from the hospital, Abbie and her mother drove all the way from San Francisco to Auburn, a journey of over one hundred miles, just to bring me a special Chinese soup that was supposed to possess amazing healing powers. Although it tasted sublime, soup was not going to cure my MS. The meal did wonders for my heart, though.

Years ago I had taken both of my sons into the kitchen and taught them to cook. Of course I had to relax that "no boys allowed" rule with which I was raised. My eldest, Dan, inherited the cooking gene from both limbs of the family tree. For a time he even considered pursuing a career in the culinary arts. However, his younger brother Patrick took what he thought would be an easier route to a life of good eats: he married a cook.

When Patrick first started dating Amanda, his older brother warned him, "Seriously dude, that woman is not a starter girlfriend." My daughter-in-law is a passionate and complicated woman, but we could tell Patrick was mesmerized by her. They met while Michael and I were living in Nashville, Tennessee. Patrick came out to visit us over Thanksgiving and when he wanted to hear some live music, Michael agreed to take him downtown. At a Nashville honky-tonk he laid eyes on the mother of my first grandchild. I don't think there is a California boy alive who can resist the charms of a Southern woman. Within six months he moved her out to the west coast.

In the early days of our relationship, Amanda and I butted heads often. However, through our common interest in all things culinary, we eventually bonded and grew to love one another. What's more, what I initially viewed as a somewhat quarrelsome nature was really just a streak of feistiness that I couldn't help but admire.

Each morning Amanda prepares a gourmet box lunch for my son to take to work. When he began repeatedly coming home with his green beans and cauliflower untouched she went into overdrive, searching for vegetable dishes that would suit his fussy palate. Despite her efforts, the plastic containers kept coming back with everything eaten except the vegetables. On the day when his boss chose to have lunch with him in the company break room, Patrick pulled his plastic container out and discovered, to his acute embarrassment, that his loving wife had sent him a message.

In black, bold letters she had scrawled across the lid of the container, *"Eat your fucking vegetables!"*

With that audacious act she managed to succeed where I had failed, converting him into a man who eats what is put in front of him. You just have to admire a woman like that.

She brings all of that spirit and drive into the kitchen. Her highly organized and comprehensive spice collection is awe-inspiring. With the fearlessness of youth she dives into even the most complex recipe without blinking an eye. She doesn't buy sausages; she makes them by hand using meat from a pig she butchered at a class she took on meat carving. She doesn't use store-bought tomato sauce: she cans her own. *This girl can cook.* My grandson, Jackson, is cutting his teeth on homemade chicken curry, ground lamb with kale and garlic, and fresh-made applesauce mixed with handpicked black-berries she harvested herself from a neighbor's field.

It is enough to bring tears to the eyes of his food fanatic of a grandmother.

A family is such a confusing, exasperating and marvelous entity. Mine is as delightfully dysfunctional as any and it took awhile to achieve our current state of relative congeniality. Along the way, there were childhoods for Michael and me that encompassed a lot of pain. Our sons suffered through the divorce of their parents in spite of our efforts to shield them from the anger and frustration of marital battles. We've endured financial and health-related ordeals, the struggles of family members with addiction issues, and painful separations brought on by misunderstandings. We are as much united by our shared sorrow as we are by our love.

My brother and I are prime examples of people who survived a difficult family situation with our sanity somewhat intact. With a cold, critical mother and an alcoholic father, we were left to essentially fend for ourselves while still in our teens. We both stumbled many times on the road to adulthood, but we also forged a bond between us that would stand as an impenetrable wall of mutual protection and devotion. There is never a doubt that my outrageous but lovable brother has my back.

Bill is truly a piece of work. He is larger-than-life and full of stories. Some of them are even true. My sons view their Uncle Bill with a mixture of awe and amusement. He has traveled from Bali to Romania, on one occasion making a brief and unplanned visit to a foreign jail. His escapades are the stuff of our more colorful family lore. With an imposing frame of nearly six foot, four inches, he doesn't merely enter a room; he fills it up entirely. His booming laugh can cause the walls to vibrate. He is fun personified. Just don't set your watch by his stated arrival time because Bill is easily distracted by shiny objects. He means well; you just learn not to hold dinner for him.

No one was surprised when Bill announced a number of years back that he was packing up and moving to New Zealand to retire at age forty-five and spend the rest of his life surfing. It was simply the latest in a long line of outlandish plans. Of course, after a few years, boredom set in and he decided he needed another adventure. During a visit with us that included a trip to the local farmers' market, he discovered kettle corn, a sweet-salty popcorn concoction. On the spot, he declared that he intended to single-handedly introduce the product to New Zealanders. True to form, he jumped into this new endeavor with total abandon, investing his life savings in the venture. Within a year, without any prior experience in food production or marketing, he became the kettle corn king of New Zealand, raking in the profits and creating a minor empire for himself and his son Ryan.

With an entire clan of great cooks, who ends up making money in the food business? My crazy brother who had never before stepped foot in a kitchen to do anything beyond pour dry cereal into a bowl.

## Menu:

### Lamb burgers
with green olive
tapenade and arugula

### Fresh summer fruit salad
with minted sugar

### Yam and Yukon Gold potato salad
with bacon and blue cheese

### Homemade gingersnaps

## Guest list:

Jen & Gary
Dan & Abbie
my brother, Bill

After years of living abroad, my brother was anxious to once again be present for that uniquely American experience of fireworks, parades and barbeque. The Fourth of July has to be one of the best holidays for a party. The weather is usually great, the food is traditionally unpretentious and the after-dinner entertainment is always thoughtfully provided by the local city officials.

Everyone arrived early for wine tasting and just hanging around Sonoma on an absolutely gorgeous summer day. In the morning, Michael and I took Bill down to the Sonoma Plaza to catch the Fourth of July parade. There can't be many that depict small town charm better. Leading the parade was the aptly titled "Hometown Band," a motley crew of mismatched musicians. The parade is a slow procession, requiring hours to complete, and allows for a "second" band (really just the first guys after some slight wardrobe changes) to bring up the rear of the parade. They are cleverly dubbed "The Other Hometown Band." The sight and sound of these townspeople enthusiastically playing patriotic music brought tears to our eyes.

Energetic Cub Scouts herded down the street by frazzled den mothers, dogs in crazy costumes pulling at their leashes, and the usual array of prancing horses and politicians waving from convertibles were all on display. It was American goofiness at its finest.

After dinner we all headed to the high school soccer field to watch the fireworks. I brought along silly 3D glasses. We may have looked like a bunch of goofballs but we had a fabulous time being wowed by the trippy pyrotechnics.

Summer parties are typically uncomplicated, relaxed events. Warm nights out in the backyard don't require fancy menus. Our gatherings had segued into laid-back, casual affairs that allowed everyone to enjoy the simple pleasures of a good burger or pizza. Shorts and flip-flops were perfectly appropriate attire.

By now I was Gandhi in the kitchen. I had finally stumbled upon the secret of being an outstanding hostess. Here is it is: Take a breath and enjoy yourself. That's all. I proved to myself, several times in fact, that you can burn the food, spill the wine and conk out before dessert, but if you and your guests are smiling as you see them to the door you've rocked the whole hostess thing. What a good hostess does not do is attempt to put on an event designed to impress foreign dignitaries. Our gatherings were about fun, laughter and good times together. They were not about fancy china, stuffy manners or showing off.

I initially fretted about achieving a spotless house every Sunday until I realized I was asking too much of myself. Would our guests be miffed if my bed was unmade? Would we have less fun if there was a little dust on a bookshelf? Of course not. I started to really enjoy our Sundays when I decided to simply do a thorough cleaning of the guest bathroom and close the doors to the rest of the rooms. It only took me twenty-six weeks to figure that out.

However, even the most confident and relaxed hostess knows lively conversation is essential. Nothing will get the guests fidgeting in their seats faster than stilted mumblings and lengthy silences. It doesn't matter what you serve, if you don't find a means of enticing your guests to talk, their dining experience will be the equivalent of eating gruel.

Each week we tried out a variety of conversation starters. One of Michael's more interesting questions was meant to elicit a conversation about who our guests admired most and why. He would ask everyone at the table to imagine intelligent life had been discovered on another planet and a three-person team was to be sent across the universe to meet them. Which three people would you select to represent the human race? You could choose anyone, even if they had been dead for centuries. Among our guests' suggestions were Abraham Lincoln, Albert Einstein, Bill Gates and Mother Teresa. But a large number of people chose celebrities. Oprah's name came up often. Some thought we should send a gorgeous starlet like Halle Berry or Marilyn Monroe to represent the more aesthetically pleasing segment of the human race.

Movie stars were not my first choice. I grew up around Hollywood. My father was a stuntman in what was referred to by the old timers as "the picture business." After a brief and not very successful career as a bronco rider on the rodeo circuit, he figured a job that would pay him to fall off the horse was right up his alley.

Each week, my brother and I would position ourselves in front of our old black-and-white television for episodes of *Maverick*, *Gunsmoke* and *Bonanza* to watch our father get shot from his saddle and die in a spectacular fashion. With his dark skin and hair, my father was usually cast in the role of an Indian. That meant he would undoubtedly be killed off sometime during the show. In a hail of bullets he and his horse would go down with a dramatic display of flailing limbs. The death scenes never failed to unnerve me.

During vacation breaks from school, my brother and I would often accompany our father to the studios to watch the filming of his stunts. I met Clint Eastwood, Paul Newman, Robert Redford and others. As I was only ten, they were nothing more to me than very nice, but boring, adults. What had my brother and me giddy with excitement was the opportunity to visit the set of the television series "Batman." Now that was entertainment! I also think Batman would be an excellent choice for that space voyage.

Another night, Michael posed a question from an article he had read about determining personality traits. You're standing on the edge of a cliff. What are you most afraid of? Falling, jumping or being pushed? Most people said they fear they'll lose their balance and fall, denoting insecurity. A few others said they were afraid someone will inexplicably push them to their death, identifying themselves as lacking trust. Finally, the smallest subset of people will consider jumping, not out of suicidal tendencies, but just to see if, against all reason, they might actually be able to fly. They, supposedly, are the dreamers, the imaginative souls among us who believe that even in the face of overwhelming odds, miracles can occur.

I didn't know how to answer the question. Anyone who had the courage to invite a crowd for dinner every Sunday would naturally be perceived as daring. In truth, I was as cowardly as they come. I didn't want to get anywhere near a cliff in the first place.

I did have flying dreams in my youth, however, and they were euphoric experiences. Some people sprout wings in their dreams; others simply rise helicopter-like into the air. I was a jumper. I needed to get up on something very high, such as a mountain or rooftop. A flash of spine-tingling doubt would always wash over me before I leaped, though. Pushing past it in expectation of that split second before the wind unfailingly elevated my body upward was where the true thrill of the experience lay. I hadn't had those dreams for a very long time.

As everyone else came up with their answers, I sat quietly and considered my lack of confidence. My life had become frozen in that moment of hesitation. I was no longer willing to trust that the updrafts would be there. So disillusioned was I with myself and the world that the notion of flying had been discarded even in my dreams.

Goals I had never met, opinions that proved to be wrong, lovers that came and went all contributed to my disenchantment with risk-taking. Of course, the biggest disillusionment of my life had been the belief that I'd always be strong and healthy. Distrust and insecurity now seemed like reasonable stances. I had back away from a cliff once, choosing not to end my life, but was there anything left of the girl who believed she could fly?

A few days later, I decided I must find the answer to that question.

"Let's go to the beach today, Michael."

"Okay. I'm in the mood for one of those crab sandwiches at the Bodega Harbor. What do you want to do?"

"I'm not sure. I might want to jump off a cliff."

"Okay, but we get the sandwiches first."

Bodega Bay is only an hour's drive from Sonoma along winding country roads that snake past pastoral farm scenes and endless stretches of vineyards. We arrived at the coastline in the early morning. The northern coast of California bears little resemblance to the postcard-perfect sandy stretches of the state's southern beaches. Massive boulders stacked by ancient earthquakes form a barrier into which the ocean incessantly slams in a futile effort to breach the coastline. Small patches of sand are constantly assaulted by angry, churning waves. There is a stark, wild beauty to the shoreline here that appeals to me in a visceral way. This is nature in all of its dangerous, unforgiving grandeur.

From rocky outlooks, you can gaze out over a watery landscape that is daunting in its vastness. When we arrived, the best viewpoints were already crowded with visitors. I waited until almost everyone had left before cautiously sidling up to the cliff's edge. Michael sat on a nearby bench calmly munching his sandwich.

I scanned the remaining people around me and determined that none looked sufficiently crazed or able-bodied enough to hoist me over the brink.

Inching toward the ledge, I took my emotional pulse. Of course, jumping was never a real consideration. My experience with suicidal thoughts after leaving the hospital had shook me to the core, but would the fantasy of flight surface from the depths of my imagination? The wind rushing up from the sea below seemed strong enough to float an elephant in mid-air. Surely it would safely buoy me, allowing for soaring flight over the jagged cliffs out to the farthest waves. I pictured myself, arms outstretched, as I let go of that last grip. A vision of that deliciously terrifying second of weightless anticipation made me gasp with the exhilaration of it. I rose up on the tips of my toes and leaned out as far as I could. No trepidation. Amazingly, I found I did not focus on the void below, only seeing the vast expanse of potential stretching out before me.

That night my bed became a towering rooftop perch and I once again felt the wind rise up to greet me. I might not be able to trust my body anymore, but I had discovered I could still trust my heart to believe in miracles.

With newfound hope, I was once again soaring in my dreams. Unfortunately, during waking hours, my body was still mired in the nightmare of MS. I was becoming increasingly numb. The areas that weren't anesthetized by my immune system were being assaulted by the same enemy with stabbing pain. There were fewer and fewer neutral zones of normality.

Your body anchors you to life. When it suddenly behaves in a confusing and self-destructive manner, you feel a profound sense of betrayal. It is shocking to realize you can't trust your own organs. Furthermore, there is no escaping from your own body; you can leave someone who hurts you, and you can quit a job that causes you frustration, but there is no getting away from a body that has turned against you. It makes sense that a heart will eventually tire from years of monotonous beating. It is understandable that if disease-carrying organisms mount an invasion against you, you'll become ill. But why would your own body make the choice to harm itself?

I was infuriated with my immune system. I always used to brag about its amazing strength; how I could stand in a room full of people with the flu and come away unscathed. Now that very same immune system had unleashed upon me some of the most powerful weapons in its arsenal, as though I were the enemy. I had been double-crossed by my own body. What's more, this was a body that had been well cared for, even pampered.

But in all honesty I had to admit I had not always been kind to this body. For most of my life, like many of my female friends, I hated how my body looks. I have openly embraced every beauty treatment, miracle cream, anti-aging elixir or cosmetic procedure that promised to transform me into someone other than the woman I saw in the mirror. I have even made numerous trips to the plastic surgeon's office. Eye lifts, laser resurfacing, liposuction, Botox…bring it on! My body in its natural state was unacceptable. I had to flog it into shape at the gym, starve it into submission with countless over-restrictive diets, and when those methods failed to work well enough, I was eager to pay thousands of dollars for someone to suck the fat out of me.

I was willing to slather hot wax on my body's most tender areas to rip out unwanted hair and, like most women, I have endured hours of dyeing, perming, crimping, hot ironing and bleaching at the beauty salon. After a lifetime of self-loathing I've undoubtedly spent enough money to buy a small island in an attempt to make my body acceptable.

Now I just hoped the damned thing would keep working.

However when a friend thoughtlessly told me I was "letting myself go," all the old feelings of inadequacy came roaring back. I knew I wasn't as fashionable as I had been before I became ill. The weakness in my limbs combined with the shakiness of my hands made it difficult to apply make-up. I had become inept at blow-drying and styling my hair. The only practical solution was to have it cut in a short, easy-to-manage style. That was a painful day. I cried as each long lock of hair hit the salon floor. And I could no longer wear high heels. Facing the fact that I would never be stable enough to safely wear them again, I packed up dozens of beautiful shoes and took them to the Goodwill store. Another tough day. But I had been proud of myself for handling these changes with at least a measure of maturity. Now, however, I was being told by this woman that accepting my new reality with grace wasn't enough. I was supposed to look chic in the process. She was one friend I no longer needed.

One day my daughter-in-law asked for a few baby pictures of her husband. Rummaging through my old cedar chest with her, I came across photos of myself through the ages. As we laughed at all the hairstyle and fashion statements I had made she said, "You were so beautiful, Mom."

Staring at the photo of a willowy girl with an achingly hopeful smile I did see a young, pretty woman. Lithe and tanned from a summer at the beach, with a wisp of thick, sun-streaked hair blowing across her face, she looked like the quintessential California girl. But that teenager in the photo certainly did not see herself as beautiful. The sixteen-year-old "me" thought she was too tall, her breasts too small, her hair too curly.

A photo of me in my twenties depicted an equally lovely but fuller, more womanly body. That version of me was aghast at the modest weight gain motherhood had brought about. Throughout my thirties and forties the story remained the same. I could never recognize the assets, but had no trouble distinguishing the numerous perceived liabilities. Only in retrospect was I able to see an attractive woman.

Now when I look down at this round, soft belly that somehow weaseled its way onto my waistline, whenever I catch sight of my image in a store window, the reflection of a much older woman than I expect to see, I am slightly appalled. I am shocked to see the brown spots that dot my hands, the graying of my temples and the tiny folds that seem to multiply daily at my neck and in the corners of my eyes.

But, if I'm lucky enough to live until my seventies or beyond that woman will look back on pictures of me taken during this era of my life. I'm quite certain what she will notice is that the woman in the photo, the one who looks like she's about to burst into laughter, is indeed attractive. She won't see a backside that's a bit broader than it used to be. She'll notice the grin, not the wrinkles. And she'll wonder why she was so hard on herself. Most of all, I'm afraid she'll look at the photo of herself walking on the beach with Bella and Michael and be dismayed that this woman ever wasted a moment of precious time worrying about such trivial concerns.

I knew it was time to finally make peace with my body. We were in this life together. Taking care of myself now meant eating right, getting as much exercise as I could handle and being gentle with myself emotionally. I still wanted to look nice, but the days of torturing my body in a vain attempt to achieve conventional beauty were over. Oddly enough I actually began to like what I was seeing in the mirror for the first time in my life. My naturally curly hair was kind of cute when allowed to just air-dry and fall in place. With a little moisturizer my skin glowed. Menopause and a lack of calorie-burning exercise had added a few pounds to my mid-section, but a summer spent in loose, flowing sundresses and flip-flops was a treat after all of those years of trying to starve myself into a bikini. Best of all, in my new natural state, Michael declared I was now prettier than I had ever been before. What a guy.

## Menu:

### Margarita pizza

### Rigatoni
with sauce Bolognese

### Chopped salad
with salami and balsamic
vinaigrette

### Pear cake
with ginger gelato

### Guest list:

Gary & Vicki
Scott & Julia
Jeanette & Dave

After thirty dinner parties, my enthusiasm was waning. But Sunday had arrived again, and I needed to get some food on the table. I decided a simple, traditional Italian dinner would do just fine. It was all I had in me. The weather had been unseasonably cool for weeks, and it seemed the perfect time to put on a big pot of sauce and let it cook all day. Unfortunately, however, by the time the guests arrived, my tiny kitchen had heated up to the temperature of a sauna. Not good for someone with MS. By the time dinner was on the table, I was as limp as the rigatoni and in pain. I didn't want to eat. I didn't want to talk. I didn't even want to be sitting at the table. After picking at my dinner a bit, I excused myself and went in to lie down. I was, in short, a horrible hostess. Thank goodness, Michael took up the slack and kept the party somewhat lively.

MS doesn't kill you. It just wears you down until dying looks like a damned fine option.

Dying is not something I had planned on doing. I know that is a ridiculous stance, but I've never been one who enjoys surprises. With all the ambiguity around death, I just can't get my head around the concept. I need a little more information before I can agree to go there. With none forthcoming—or at least none I'm willing to accept as reliable—I have chosen to simply ignore the possibility. It might help if I were able to believe that a benevolent deity was waiting out there somewhere, willing to welcome me into that great party in the sky, but I've never been the type to suspend my natural tendency to question concepts that seem a little too good to be true. I was the kid who couldn't get past the fake beard while sitting on Santa's lap.

My life is not devoid of principles; it is merely god-free. I take pride in the fact that my moral compass is not predicated on a reward system. I simply can't swallow the theory that doing the right thing will earn me bonus mileage in the hereafter or that a scary guy in the sky will smite the hell out of me if I don't. However, treating others with respect does seem like the prudent path to take if I hope to be thought of fondly after I am gone or, more importantly, while I am here.

Some Sundays our gathering table buzzed around the topic of religion with an intensity that was invigorating. Just because I'm not a fan of organized worship doesn't mean I don't respect and love a number of people who are believers. When our religious and atheistic friends realized that faith was not a taboo topic at our dinners, the chatter at the table turned to animated and passionate deliberations that were enthralling to witness. Both sides realized a goal of converting was not only useless but tiresome, so the discussions seemed to move quickly past that into the realm of honest debate. We wrestled with the concept of life after death, the origin of evil, and the purpose of human existence over plates of steaming pasta. Everyone began these conversations by taking great pains to present their opinions in a respectful manner, while at the same time gauging the interest of others in some cordial philosophical sparring. After the niceties, forks became tools of expression, waving fervently to punctuate salient points.

I adore and respect my church-going friends, and I know they accept and love me, the hell-bound sinner in their midst. My dear friend Stacia, an ardent Baptist, called me from Tennessee when she first learned of my illness and hospitalization.

"Bless your heart, what happened to you?" she drawled.

"I think my warranty has expired. I should have purchased that extended plan."

"Well, I called the pastor at church and we've organized a prayer circle for you."

"Stacia thanks so much but that's not necessary. I hate to think of all of those nice church ladies wasting their breath over me."

"Hush. And just do me one favor…don't put up that heathen shield of yours to block them!"

I wouldn't have dared. You don't mess with a Southern Baptist congregation from the Bible belt. Besides, when someone is offering to employ her deeply held and sacred beliefs in an effort to help you, the least you can do is be sincerely grateful. It is one thing to hold a strong opinion, but it is quite another to allow your stance to veer into the realm of arrogance.

While I may have wished it was possible to opt out of the whole dying business, the in-your-face quality of a progressive disease doesn't allow you to deny your own gradual disintegration. The very real possibility that in the future I might need someone to change my diaper for me is far more distressing than death. A sudden, lights-out exit is much more palatable. Of course a degenerative condition doesn't exclude the possibility of an accident, but odds are my demise will be a measured march downward. How far I was willing to go was a question I wasn't yet ready to address.

Since having been diagnosed, I've believed Michael would probably outlive me. Or at least I sincerely hoped that would be the case and I was determined to do everything in my power to ensure he did. I became a vigilant guardian of his well-being. A healthy diet, regular exercise and a relatively stress-free life were things I could help him to achieve. If my own health was already a bust, at least I could attempt to maintain his.

I could not imagine how I could endure the ravages of this disease without his strength. I knew perfectly well the source of much of my courage was sitting across from me each night at dinner. Adjusting to the dependency that comes with a chronic condition is difficult for both partners. I had a husband who had learned from his father about devotion and dependability. He knew all about remaining steadfast in the face of MS, but he also knew exactly how grim the trials we were facing might become. I could choose to remain blissfully in denial: he would have to shoulder the task of being realistic.

During our tumultuous dating years, I had urged Michael to go with me to a therapist in order to overcome his fear of commitment. In that session he finally admitted it wasn't a fear of commitment that was keeping him from letting go of his heart. It was a fear of my death.

He told the therapist that when his mother died he made a promise he would never put himself in a position to experience that much emotional pain again. He said, "If I let myself love Ronda I'm afraid she'll get sick and die. And I can't bear to lose two women I love." At the time I had scoffed at his concern. I was a very healthy woman. Nothing bad would happen to me.

I loved him for his devotion, but I also sometimes felt crushed with guilt. It was my unreasonable body that was causing all this grief. Our happiness, our security, the very quality of our lives was being diminished by my illness. On some level it felt as though all of this misery was my fault and I could do absolutely nothing to change things. There was no health regimen, no exercise routine, no diet I could adhere to that would halt this downward spiral.

But evidently there was plenty of self-reproach to go around. Michael once confessed that he sometimes felt an overwhelming sense of survivor guilt. Watching me suffer, he irrationally felt he was to blame. This was supposed to be his fate, not mine. But given the opportunity, I'm quite sure I would not choose to switch places with him. I've seen the look of helpless desperation on his face as I battled to stay on top of excruciating pain. I get all of the sympathy and concern. He gets the responsibility. I'm allowed to wail. He stays steadfastly calm. Ironically, I'm certain he would valiantly switch places. He would lift this burden off of me in a minute if he could. He's that kind of a man. But of course, that was not an option. I would be the victim of this disease and he would be my companion and ally in the journey. Neither of us had the easier role.

As odd as it sounds, I must admit I've never fully accepted the possibility that this will end badly. My son Dan once accused me of being so optimistic that I view a glass as not merely half full but miraculously overflowing. Perhaps that is my personal defense system. I am aware that most people in my situation will not fare well, but somehow I expect to be the exception to the rule.

An optimistic personality can get you far in life, but it can also cloud your judgment. Every time I suffered another severe pain attack, I tried to convince myself it was the last one. After all, the tremors had subsided and I had regained control of my hands. I no longer needed a cane to steady myself. "This too shall pass" was my motto. But as the summer drew to a close, the attacks started occurring more and more often. It was increasingly difficult to deny that pain had, in fact, become a permanent feature of my life. Living with it was now the objective. As much as I wanted to believe I could simply cook my way through this, I knew there were some problems even a nice day in the kitchen could not solve.

After months of waiting I was finally able to get an appointment with a physician who specialized in pain management. My goal was to find a means of coping with the agony and most of all to avoid any more trips to the emergency room.

I hate emergency rooms. They have to be some of the most dreadful and unpleasant places on earth. With our repeated visits over the past months, Michael and I had racked up more than a hundred hours in the chaos and misery of emergency rooms. Each trip began with a brief period of sheer panic followed by endless hours of mind-numbing boredom. I would arrive writhing in pain, begging for help. Thankfully, after the first couple of times I showed up at their door, the compassionate ER staff recognized me and would quickly usher me into my own little curtained cubicle to receive an IV for the pain medication. But then came the waiting. If a decision was made to admit me to the hospital, Michael and I were in for a long, tedious tenure in that cubicle. The most dreaded words a patient in the ER can hear are, "We're trying to find a bed for you." That process can take up to twelve hours on a bad day. In the meantime, you lie on a gurney listening to the agony of those around you. Groans, tears, and tortured retching are the background "music." Emergency rooms exist in another time dimension. "Someone will be right in" can mean a wait of anything from a few minutes to several hours. With no clock and no window to the outside world, time slows to a crawl.

In spite of my pleas for him to escape the insanity of that place, Michael would never leave my side. We were in this together. He always patiently waited for the attendant to deliver me to the relative peace of a hospital room before he headed home to grab a little sleep. And the next morning he would always appear in my room with a big smile, some special treat, and his assurances that all would be well.

It was perhaps inevitable, however, that Michael occasionally experienced moments when he wanted to walk away from the drama. How could I fault him for those rare days when he could not summon the patience and resolve to handle yet another crisis?

Unfortunately, those lapses left me with a terrifying awareness of my growing vulnerability.

It was a fiercely hot summer day when we arrived in Napa for a party celebrating the opening of a chic new winery. It was supposed to be a special treat, a chance to revel in the luxurious paradise of the wine country. We were all decked out in our swankiest summer outfits and anticipating an abundance of gourmet food and fine wines. Unfortunately, we encountered a line at the entrance to the event stretching almost to the parking lot. I could feel the strength seeping out of my limbs as each minute in the unmerciful heat ticked on. By the time we finally reached the relative coolness of the lawn, my legs had become so wobbly I was forced to hold firmly to Michael's arm to remain upright.

As my grip tightened, I could see tension hardening his features. "Not again!" were the words that seemed ready to burst from him. With no chairs in sight, he led me to a shaded area in an out-of-the-way corner where I could at least prop myself up against a small table.

"I need to talk to a couple of clients. Will you be alright?"

"Yes, of course," I said with a breezy tone that rang false even to my ears.

"I'm sorry, but I really need to speak to these people."

"I know. Just go, okay? I'm fine. I'll wait here for you."

Fine was exactly what I was determined to be. I was adamant that this situation was not going to spiral into another disaster. But even firm resolve is sometimes no match for MS. Michael had been gone only minutes when my legs began to weaken.

Panic had my blood pumping at a furious rate, swelling the muscles in my thighs and tightening them into hard columns of resistance against the sway of the earth beneath me. As my toes curled downward in a desperate attempt to grip the ground through the soles of my shoes, I widened my stance and forced myself to measure out breaths in slow, calming inhalations and exhalations. With a brain that was issuing distress signals in an increasingly shrill tone, I attempted to assemble an honest assessment of my diminishing options. I sensed my opportunities for a graceful exit from the event were becoming increasingly slim.

I might have had a remote shot at successfully traversing the forty yards or so of lawn between me and Michael. The price of failure, however, would be a very public tumble and the ensuing drama it would undoubtedly trigger. Someone would probably call 9-1-1, crowds would gather around. I would become a spectacle. Worst of all, the general assumption would be that I had committed one of the most grievous of social sins in the Napa Valley: getting sloppy drunk at a posh winery affair.

If I actually managed to stay on my feet, a lurching, inelegant stagger across the expanse would certainly be viewed with just as much disdain on the part of the crowd clustered around the appetizers and wine pouring stations. If I fell on my ass I could at least explain my condition.

I had a clear view of Michael across the expanse of grass and well-dressed guests. The sight of his animated gestures and wide grin told me that I was the last thing on his mind. While time was racing towards disaster for me, he seemed to be thoroughly enjoying a leisurely conversation and a respite from his wreck of a spouse. I hated him at that moment. I despised the way he casually stood, wineglass in hand, throwing back his head in laughter at some witty remark.

Even if I were to attempt an ill-mannered shout across the garden, I was certain he would not hear me. All I could do was hurl vile mental messages his way, willing him to look in my direction. If he was picking up my psychic signals, he was pointedly ignoring them. I was forced to wait until he recalled he had a pitiful wife who was about to sink unceremoniously into a heap in the grass.

Of course he hadn't actually forgotten me. But I'm certain he was aware he was lingering longer than necessary, that he had stepped off the path for some much-needed normalcy.

He would always be able to walk away from this. I didn't have that luxury. Then an even more chilling thought occurred to me. What if this disease progressed to the point where I was permanently helpless, and parked in a corner unable to move without his assistance? And what would I do if he chose to leave me there?

Fear, anxiety and heat were all closing in on me, threatening to break through my last thread of self-control when I finally spotted him walking toward me. One look at my face, pale and slick with perspiration, and he knew the whole story. He jogged the final few feet to me and quickly offered the security of his embrace.

"I'm so sorry. I lost track of time."

What he lost track of was me. For those brief twenty minutes, torturously long for me, he was a man free of obligations; I was a feeble and needy woman. If this was our future, we were doomed. In the car on the way home I tried to explain my concerns, to tell him how terrifying it was to imagine becoming a burden.

"There was a time when my father began to feel that caring for my mother and two small sons was more than he could handle," Michael began. "He decided the best solution was to find a nursing home for her."

I could feel my stomach shrinking into a tight ball of fear.

"We took her there on a Saturday morning. I'll never forget the tears streaming down her face as we turned and left her sitting in her wheelchair. I cried all the way home. I think I was only about eleven or twelve years old. I begged my dad to go back and get her. The next day he relented. When we walked in the door she was in exactly the same spot as we had left her. It about broke my dad's heart. Nobody mentioned putting her in a nursing home ever again. But my dad did ask her to help him. He needed her to smile more, to try and remain optimistic so he could stay strong."

"I'll smile more, Michael."

"That's all I need, Ronda. I get it. I really do. This is hard for both of us, but we'll get through it. You just have to keep that great attitude of yours. And you have to keep believing in me. I promise I won't ever leave you. *Ever*. No matter how bad things get."

I reached for his hand. I would never again wonder whether he would come back for me.

During our first meeting with him, the pain management doctor told us I had a particular form of MS that would probably always include pain. The news caused us both to sink a little lower in our chairs. He informed us we could expect the attacks to occur closer and closer together until they were almost a daily occurrence. That prospect was perhaps the most chilling we had heard yet. How could I possibly have a life that included joy and laughter if I was constantly in pain? He assured us that he would work with me to find a pain medication that would control the attacks and still allow me to function. Best of all, we could safely use the medication at home and would not require another agonizing trip to the emergency room. With that assurance and a prescription for liquid morphine, we left his office feeling like we at least had a measure of power over the situation. A mere week later, when another attack came, Michael reached for the morphine and we both waited for it to take effect. When the pain kept building with no relief in sight, we had to concede defeat and rush, once again, to the dreaded hospital. We were back on the phone with him the next day to find another solution.

The doctor gave us another prescription and told us not to worry. He had been successful in alleviating pain for all of his MS patients except one. This unfortunate woman was unable to find relief through any medication. Knocking her nearly unconscious was the only answer.

Her fate haunted me. And Michael, too, I'm certain.

*When* the world says, "Give up,"
Hope whispers, "Try it one more time."

**~Author Unknown**

*five*

With Sunday only a day away I had to make a difficult decision. Was over six months of gatherings enough? Did I have it in me to pull out the cookbook and muster up my resolve for one more round of guests?

We had dozens of wonderful Sundays in our memory. Did we really need more? I was so tired much of the time now. And Michael's work was increasingly challenging as the economy thinned the ranks of visitors to the wine country. What we needed was a long restful Sunday. What did I do? I accepted a record number of guests and we spent an evening drinking excellent wine until we were, as they say in the South, "a bit in our cups." With the turntable churning out the tunes of our youth, Michael and I were able to forget what might lie ahead. What a wonderful night. I made the right decision.

## Menu:

### Pizza
with salmon, red onion and
goat cheese

### Grilled lamb
over lemon risotto with
baby artichokes

### Romaine with fresh
### dill, feta, cucumbers and
### garden tomatoes

### Apple raisin tart
with crème fraiche

### Guest list:

Michael & Brian
Vance & Monika
Mike & Phyllis
Scott & Brett
Richard

Michael is the consummate host. Throughout the year he reveled in his role as chief greeter, sommelier and deejay. His prized possession is a collection of record albums from the sixties and seventies. With hundreds of them, he was always ready to play a guest's favorite song from the past. A constant feature of our gatherings was the music that emanated from a twenty-year-old turntable Michael had rescued from a friend's garage and placed center stage in our home.

For years, I had fought a battle to remove the stacks of old record albums that were ruining my decorating scheme for the living room. I tried purchasing snazzy woven boxes and attempted to hide the unsightly things from view. No luck. The two of us were locked in a perpetual battle of wills, with Michael removing the albums and stacking them on top of the boxes and me coming behind him to put them out of sight again. Finally, I realized this was a fight I'd never win. Better to simply defect to the enemy camp and attempt to wrangle some control over the ever-increasing piles of dusty albums. For his birthday I surprised him with a pair of stylish cabinets to flank his cherished turntable. They were specifically made to display record albums and were actually quite attractive. I then meticulously alphabetized the records by recording artist. He was thrilled. With a little creative thinking, I had managed both to delight my husband and to create, as they say on the decorating shows, a nice focal point.

My new system also allowed our guests to easily peruse the collection and pick out favorites. Our buddy Mike, a true rock 'n' roll original, especially enjoyed the albums. He also held the distinction of being our only guest to have a recording of sorts on one of them. As the former public relations manager for the Allman Brothers Band, he possesses a wealth of stories about some of the biggest names in the music industry. He also created a tiny bit of legacy for himself on the album, *The Allman Brothers Band Live at Fillmore East*. Over the roar of the music Mike's voice can be heard shouting out the words, "Play all night!" It only constituted about five seconds of fame, but we were impressed nonetheless.

On several nights my husband posed the question, "What was your favorite make-out album when you were a teenager?" That prompted our guests to take turns searching through the collection to find the music that sparked their early love affairs. I have a feeling more than a few of them ducked out early to go home and enjoy a romantic interlude prompted by those old memories.

## Menu:

### Pizza
with Yukon Gold potatoes, fresh rosemary and slivered prosciutto

### Sicilian-style grilled tilapia

### Pasta salad
with fresh mozzarella, tomatoes, capers and basil

### Caesar salad

### Homemade ginger shortcakes
with fresh peach gelato

### Guest list:

Sue & Wayne
Terry & Cully
Cynthia
Karen

I certainly never expected to complete this challenge when I started it in January, but as time went on I began to realize it just might happen. The finish line wasn't quite in sight, but I began to believe I might one day reach it.

If I could count on all the remaining Sunday dinners being as idyllic as this one, I would have no problem finishing out the year. I started the morning with a cup of cappuccino, thoughtfully provided by my husband, and *The New York Times*. I then flipped on the computer and began perusing the recipe sites for some ideas about a menu. I came up with Sicilian Grilled Fish as a main course. I made a sauce of olive oil, lemon, garlic, Italian parsley and oregano. After brushing one side of the fish with the sauce, I rolled each piece up tightly. I then poured on the remaining sauce, topped them with more lemons and wrapped it all in foil. Simple, elegant and very tasty.

For the appetizer I made an old standby, Yukon gold potato and rosemary pizza, but added prosciutto for a little flair. It was delicious. We had just gotten back from a trip to Santa Barbara and while there I found some black-and-white striped pasta. I used it for a pasta salad. For dessert, I made fresh peach gelato with ginger shortcakes. Damn, it was good. The wine flowed, the food received many compliments, and we all had a wonderful time.

Best of all, we enjoyed some marvelous conversation with our guests. Bouncing from one topic to the next, under a star-lit sky, we talked until we were all drowsy and spent, but thoroughly grateful for the amazing good fortune that had landed us in this very special corner of the world.

There is little doubt that the atmosphere we created allowed everyone to feel safe in sharing some very personal and heartfelt memories. But not every topic presented brought about insightful conversations. In spite of our best efforts, sometimes the discussions just fell flat. Maybe it was the mix of guests, perhaps it was just the tone of the night, but a few times over the year, the general mood of the night was, simply put, a bit dull.

We were blessed with a huge and ever growing army of interesting friends, so it wasn't their fault. You can prepare a marvelous meal, set a stunning table and pour some great wine but sometimes you just can't make a party. During my brief career as a stand-up comedienne I discovered dialogue that usually had the audience weak with laughter could sometimes be received with a stunned silence. Those were painful moments to say the least.

Asking provocative questions of our guests, however, usually proved to be an effective means of getting the conversation flowing. A question that elicited some riveting responses was "What was one of your most frightening experiences?"

"I'll never forget the pure hatred in his eyes," Karen told us, beginning her tale.

She and her late husband were boarding a plane in Arizona when she noticed a group of men behaving strangely, standing apart from the other travelers and whispering to one another in angry tones.

"I told my husband, but he insisted they were probably a sports team, nothing sinister about them. Besides, there hadn't been a plane hijacked in years."

As she made her way down the aisle she discovered she was seated directly behind the man who appeared to be the leader of the group. Their eyes met and his cold stare sent chills through her.

"I literally shook with fear throughout that flight."

Three weeks later she watched her television screen in horror as the Twin Towers fell.

"Later they flashed a series of photos of the terrorists. Suddenly I was staring at that face again. When I spoke to the FBI a few weeks later, I learned our flight had been one of their practice runs." We were taken aback by her brush with such evil.

Another question that often prompted heartfelt responses from even our more reserved dinner guests was "What was your most memorable kiss?" The caveat was that the story could not be about your partner or spouse. The question wasn't necessarily meant to produce salacious responses. In fact, nearly every time it was asked it drew out both poignant and comical stories.

Our neighbor, Chris once told us of the time he broke up with his college sweetheart. Their relationship had simply run its course, but the parting was proving to be painful and confrontational.

"We had argued throughout the evening and were thoroughly exasperated with each other, storming off in opposite directions. I knew it was over for good this time."

Suddenly, however, she turned and ran back to him. Holding his face in her hands, without saying a word, she simply kissed him.

"And I never saw her again. Just a few days later she was killed in a car accident. If she hadn't run back and kissed me, I don't know if I would have been able to get over her death. I would have blamed myself forever. That one last kiss helped put the heartbreak behind me so that I could eventually find love again with my wife Alicia."

We sat in stunned silence remembering last kisses and lost loves of our own.

The mood quickly changed that night, however, when our friend Terry took her turn at answering the question. She related a hilarious story of a long, late-night drive with her husband Cully at the wheel. When chatter about kids and business concerns began to fail as a means of keeping his mind on the road, she decided to try a new approach to make sure he remained wide awake. She told him that she had a confession about something that happened during her college days.

"I started to make up this story that just kept getting spicier as it went along about a stolen kiss. Not a word of it was true, but it sure was doing the job. Suddenly he was sitting up real straight with his eyes wide open. I don't know what came over me, but once I got going with that story my imagination really took off."

With Cully providing an impression of his astonishment we were weak with laughter.

"And just when I thought I knew everything about my wife," Cully chimed in. "That's what is so wonderful about marriage. After decades together you still occasionally surprise the hell out of one another."

It was clear that our stories were not just entertaining tales. They were the accompanying narrative to the lessons that we had learned along the way. From our individual cache of memories, we framed our lives for one another, the frightening moments, the touching, and the comical.

Gathered around the table, savoring that last glass of wine, we shared our opinions, our fears, and our tall tales. Best of all, we discovered we had more in common with each other than we had ever known.

# September 5th – Gathering number thirty-six

## Menu:

### Pizza
with salmon, red onion and goat cheese

### Grilled lamb
over lemon risotto with baby artichokes

### Romaine with
fresh dill, feta, cucumbers and garden tomatoes

### Homemade donuts
with Bailey's Irish Cream and coffee

## Guest list:

Donna & Larry
Vance & Monika
Steve & Molly

When my friend Donna, a master baker, signed up with her husband to attend one of our gatherings I wanted to make a dessert that would really impress her. In her honor I would attempt to recreate the magnificent gourmet donuts we had ordered during a recent dinner at a fancy restaurant. At least that's what I was telling myself. True confession: I'm a donut junkie. This one was for me.

I am addicted to donuts. They are the chink in my culinary armor. I've had to go nearly cold turkey, averting my eyes whenever I drive by a donut shop. Just one and I'm on a downward slide to obesity. I can tell myself that half of one little éclair and I'll be satisfied. But that's a lie. The other half will call to me with such persuasiveness I'll soon have pastry in hand. Then its friends, the maple bars and fritters, the crullers and warm, glazed donuts will strike up the chorus. In no time, I will have consumed a dozen of the evil things.

But when Michael and I spent a marvelous evening at an elegant restaurant in Lake Tahoe and I found fresh made donuts on the dessert menu, I decided I could risk ordering them. After all, I had a spotter. I would never have the guts to place a second order in front of a witness.

My decision to prepare donuts in my own kitchen was a risky endeavor on several fronts. First, I had never tried to make them before and deep frying is not a cooking technique I often use. But the most perilous aspect of the decision was that I might actually succeed in producing delicious donuts. Then I'd have to just throw away my jeans and head to the big girls' clothing store for tent dresses. Life as a rotund woman would be right around the corner.

Fortunately I was about to discover just how difficult it is to make a good donut. I thought that, armed with a recipe from Michael Chiarello's cookbook, I would easily produce the sweet, fluffy concoctions of my dreams. After all, he had not failed me once this entire year.

I started early in the day so I wouldn't be rushed. The dough came together with relative ease. I had purchased a deep fryer thermometer to ensure I had the oil at the proper temperature and laid out paper towels and my baking rack to cool the donuts. The first batch filled the kitchen with an aroma that nearly made me swoon. Quality control tasting was, of course, required. With just a little dusting of cinnamon and sugar, they were the epitome of perfection. I finished the rest of the frying and put them safely out of sight in a plastic container to await their presentation at the end of the meal. Unfortunately I didn't know the basic rule of donut production. Freshness is everything. Only a couple of hours of shelf time will turn them into inedible doorstops.

After a lively conversation about religion and the origin of evil, we were ready for something sweet. I proudly brought out my donuts along with a wonderfully spiked coffee drink. The silence around the table was deafening as each of our guests attempted to gnaw their way through those awful donuts. I was mortified.

But the real humiliation came when I learned that Donna's parents and brother and uncle - basically her entire family - owned donut shops. Oh well, she is a forgiving soul. She and Larry probably laughed the entire way home.

## Menu:

### Wild mushroom pizza
with smoked Gouda
and rosemary

### Field greens
with mandarin
orange vinaigrette

### Grilled salmon
with baby artichokes and
Saffron risotto

### Pear tart
with vanilla gelato

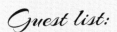

### Guest list:

Dee & Ed
Sandi & Fred
Randy & Lindsey

In spite of the cheery welcome guests received at my door, entertaining had lost a lot of its appeal. I was tired and in pain much of the time and just plain over the whole idea. The scheme had been audacious from the beginning, and I never thought I'd be well enough to complete it anyway. However, as the months passed and I was still walking, it was starting to appear that I might actually be able to pull off this stunt.

It had started out innocently enough with a simple vow to cook dinner every Sunday and for most of the year we had both gotten a kick out of the parade of parties. However, it was slowly dawning on me that I had painted myself into quite a corner.

I'm a person who looks strong out of the gate. Unfortunately I'm dogged with a reputation for fizzling out before reaching the finish line. My ex-husband once chivalrously suggested that I should be sequestered in a room with a nice comfy chair so I could do nothing but think of cool stuff. I'm great with ideas, just lousy with follow-through.

Leaving this project unfinished, however, would be a very public failure. By now nearly one hundred people had attended one of our dinners and many more had heard about them. My little blog was getting more hits every week. Thanks to the Internet, my story was being passed from person to person. I was inundated with e-mails from people I had never met who were cheering me on from the sidelines. I also received poignant messages from others who were suffering from MS, as well as from cancer and other life-threatening ailments. It was humbling to read of their trials, most much more challenging than mine, and to realize I was providing some small bit of inspiration. These people were counting on me to complete the challenge. Of course if I became seriously ill, no one would fault me for quitting, but just bailing out of irritability seemed downright cowardly.

To make matters worse, one of our guests had called a local newspaper and told the editor about my endeavors. Soon after a reporter contacted me and asked if she could write a feature story on my fifty-two dinners. Honored, I impulsively agreed to have the reporter attend a dinner in December as one of our guests. Now I really had to finish.

But I wanted out of the commitment. I didn't want to cook one more dinner. The effort required to smile was becoming increasingly exhausting. I was a crabby, mean-tempered, sick woman trapped in the body of a perky hostess.

The fact that I was still physically upright didn't mean much. I was on my knees mentally. My so-called great attitude was crumbling. Depression was closing in on me and the last thing I wanted was to be around other people.

As the doctor had predicted, the pain attacks were coming more frequently. I mentally doubled over every time I imagined an existence dominated by chronic pain. How could I find pleasure in a life that consisted of constant agony? Stumbling through my days in a drugged stupor didn't seem a viable option either.

The only course of action was to throw myself into auto-pilot. With no exit in sight, no direction that led to anything better, all I could do was keep trudging forward. Perhaps no one would notice that I was feigning happiness.

In an act that many might consider insane, I chose not to organize just a party; I put together a huge Halloween bash. If a small gathering couldn't banish the blues, maybe a big one could pull me up from the depths.

# October 31st – Gathering number forty-four

## Menu:

**Pumpkin fondue**
with toasted baguettes

**Grilled chicken**

**apple sausages**

**Lamb burger sliders**

**Stuffed mushrooms**

**Witch's broom cookies**

**Devil's food cake**
with dark chocolate frosting

## Guest list:

Tom & Anita
Jean & Doug
Jen & Gary
Mike & Phyllis
Barbara & Bob
Marc & Michelle
Chris & Alicia

After residing for years in housing communities and condo complexes that were essentially devoid of anyone under the age of forty, we were tickled about the prospect of finally having trick-or-treaters on our doorstep. Our little neighborhood is teeming with children.

I was a little concerned that our gathering might hamper our ability to fully enjoy the kids and their costumes, so I decided to pass on a sit-down dinner and have a buffet-style meal instead. I also added one more twist to this Sunday's party. Our guests were required to come in a costume. I was a little worried that the ruling might cause our friends to forego the invitation to join us at a more dignified dinner on a later date. However, I evidently grossly overestimated the level of decorum in our social circle. I received so many e-mails from friends who wanted to be included in the frivolity that I feared we'd pack our tiny house to capacity.

But just getting a houseful of costumed characters wasn't the goal. I wanted kids, lots of them. I asked our guests to skip their usual contribution of a nice bottle of wine and instead bring a box of full-sized candy bars. No puny "snack sized" treats were going to be handed out at our house this year. Others could offer pencils and granola bars. We were putting out the good stuff. I got the neighborhood kids to pass around the news bulletin: enormous Snickers, Almond Joys and Butterfingers at the Giangreco's.

Our buddy Scott donated boxes of Halloween decorations from his previous parties and I blanketed the house in spider webs, black netting and spooky ghosts. Michael grumbled as he sat next to a skull at the breakfast table, but I knew he'd get into the spirit of things as soon as he put on his costume. We both had all the regalia to transform ourselves into awesomely fierce pirates. Sophie and Luc, the twins next door, had also decided to be pirates and were delighted we'd be the adult versions. Even Bella got a pirate's scarf and hat, but she flatly refused to let me attach a fake parrot to her collar.

I had a hard time recognizing some of our guests. Barbara had to speak before I realized the lion before me was actually Bob's wife. And Mike did a perfect imitation of Uncle Fester from the *Adamm's Family*. The award for creativity, however, went to our young lawyer friends. Gary was a plug and his wife Jen came as a light socket.

As expected, we were inundated with kids. Carloads from surrounding neighborhoods poured out into the streets and swarmed around our house. We were happily overrun with superheroes and witches. A pint-sized Superman strolled right past me at the front door to check out the buffet. After surveying the adult offerings, he turned and headed back out for more trick-or-treating. One of our guests called after him "Be careful out there, Superman!" to which this rather staid little three-year-old huffily responded, "It's a just costume, lady."

For one bright fall night I was not a patient. I was a pirate. My home was filled with the laughter of friends. A parade of delightful children made its way to my front door. It was a very good Halloween.

Smiling through the tears wasn't a bad strategy for brief periods, but when the crowds left and I was alone with the rubble of the night's frivolity, despondency descended again like a dark blanket. I doubt any of our friends had any clue of just how low I had sunk.

Not even Michael's love, my sons' concern or Bella's devotion could offset the misery. The companionship of friends was no longer the healing balm it had once been.

The issue of how much pain I was willing to live with was constantly on my mind. And of course the larger question was what would I do when it reached an unbearable level? Could I pull the trigger, make the jump, swallow that last pill? I doubted it. And therein resided my greatest fear. I'm the kind of person who always bets on the long-shot. With the rose colored glasses firmly in place, would I endure intolerable pain until my last breath? Ditching the farcically upbeat point of view seemed like a move toward sanity, not a cop out, anymore.

I don't recall anyone ever commenting on my great attitude before I became disabled. Nor, to my knowledge, did my friends ever use the word courageous in reference to me. However, with the diagnosis of MS I was thrust into the role of a brave woman who would fight this disease with dignity. And the whole act was wearing thin.

If I chose to stop cooking these dinners no one would question my decision. Plus, I reasoned, it would be an act of kindness to not inflict my growing cynicism on our friends. It would be easy to back out gracefully. After all, I could lay claim to any one of several valid excuses. Sympathy would abound and even though I wouldn't make it to the end of the year, all of our friends would nonetheless congratulate me on a valiant effort.

I had to admit to myself, however, that there was no reason to quit. I knew I could do this; the pain had not reached that dreaded unbearable level yet. It was still just hovering at a damned unpleasant one.

If I gave up, I would be shamelessly using my illness as an excuse. And even if no one suspected the truth, I would have to live with the knowledge I had numbly accepted defeat. I hurt like hell at times. I was scared and tired. But I also knew I had it in me to see this thing through. It didn't matter that no one would deem me a failure. I would know I had quit before MS forced my hand. I would have allowed the disease to win the battle.

Maybe true bravery lies in that one moment in your life when you don't allow yourself to take the easy way out.

I couldn't best MS. It was impossible to cure myself with any drug or treatment plan. But, damn it, I could still cook a couple more dinners. I'd seize the one victory I knew I could still wrestle out of all this.

Thank goodness I didn't give up, because as I rounded the club house turn, the cheers began in earnest. Friends sent e-mails, notes of encouragement and jostled to get on the guest list for one of the final dinners. There were many who had, for one reason or another, been unable to make one of the Sundays earlier in the year but didn't want to miss out on being a part of our adventure. We filled the guest list to capacity each Sunday to accommodate them. By November all the slots were taken through the end of the year.

But in late October, I received a phone call from a good friend asking if we could find room for just one extra guest.

# Menu:

### Homemade ricotta
with freshly baked bread

### Roasted pork tenderloin
with homemade applesauce
with browned butter
and rosemary

### Romaine
with goat cheese, pecans
and cherry tomatoes

### Pear tart
with crème fraiche

## Guest list:

Sharyn & Bob
Terry & Cully
Kathy & Dennis
Jimmy

We had never met her brother Jimmy but we learned from our friend Phyllis that he had just recently lost his wife after a fierce battle with cancer. She told us he wasn't sure if he was ready for a social engagement but he really wanted to be a part of our adventure. We couldn't possibly say no. Unfortunately, in the commotion of the next few weeks, I completely forgot about the phone call. When Sunday night arrived, I had the table set for eight and all of our guests held their first glass of wine. Suddenly, I heard the front door open and there stood a man holding a bottle of wine in each hand. I didn't have the slightest idea who he was, but at least he looked friendly. He must have seen the confusion on my face.

"My sister told you I was coming, didn't she?" That jarred my memory.

"Of course! We're so glad you're here."

I quickly pulled Michael aside.

"As inconspicuously as possible, get a chair from the bedroom and squeeze in another place-setting at the table."

I kept Jimmy distracted with appetizers and a glass of wine while Michael discreetly rearranged the dinner table. After the guests were seated, the lively conversations swirled around our gathering table. Jimmy sat quietly just listening in. Finally, he spoke.

"I didn't think I could do this…come out and be with people. But I was tired of being alone, tired of crying."

No one but Michael and I had been told of his wife's death. Immediately the entire group offered sympathy, encouragement and empathetic stories of the losses they had endured. It was one of the most compassionate and touching evenings of our year. The tenderness of these people, all strangers to one another before that night, was beautiful to witness. And if I had given up and quit the week before I would have missed it. I wouldn't question again why I was going to the trouble and expense of preparing dinner every Sunday night. I would cherish every meal that remained.

*November 14th – Gathering number forty-six*

*Menu:*
*Ricotta with*
homemade bread

*Handmade ravioli*
with meat sauce

*Romaine salad*
with balsamic vinaigrette

*Olive oil cake*
with ice cream

*Guest list:*
Marc & Michelle
Sue & Alan
Bill & Scott

Michael and I have birthdays in November that are just five days apart. We decided we would designate a Sunday dinner to celebrate the dates, as well as those of our friends who also had birthdays this month. My brother Bill is an October baby, but he was visiting all the way from New Zealand, so we invited him to join us. Our buddy Scott wanted to have some birthday cake, so we said he could come, too.

I let Michael chose the menu. Not surprisingly, he picked ravioli. Because spending the day in the kitchen was exactly how I wanted to celebrate my birthday, I agreed. An entire day was needed to make ricotta, roll out ravioli, bake bread, get a nice hearty sauce simmering on the stove and bake a cake. Thankfully I was in good shape, with no pain and no fatigue, even though the twin evils had been plaguing me all week. Evidently the MS monster was willing to cut me some slack on my birthday.

Years ago, after Michael had given me a birthday gift of floor mats for my car, I declared we would no longer exchange gifts. I would buy my own and I would not be shopping at the auto parts store. However, I told him that at least once in my life I wanted a surprise party. I told my friend Sue about my request and she confessed she too had hoped to come home one day and find a house full of friends and balloons. We laughed thinking about the improbability of our husbands executing such a party. And we simultaneously made a silent vow to start planning one for each other.

I swear I had no idea as I was getting ready for a birthday lunch with Sue, that a dozen of my girlfriends were gathering at her house to surprise me. What a thrill! After I got over the shock, I just stood there and cried. It had taken fifty-six years, but I finally got my surprise party. It was especially sweet because I knew in just over a week I'd be returning the favor with the help of another friend. Believe it or not, Sue was just as surprised.

Who would have guessed the year that was supposed to be my worst would be the year in which I enjoyed the best birthday of my life?

*I have heard there are troubles of more than one kind.Some come from ahead and some come from behind.  But I've bought a big bat.  I'm all ready you see.  Now my troubles are going to have troubles with me!*

**~Dr. Seuss**

six

With the finish line in sight Michael and I discussed how to celebrate the completion of fifty-two dinner parties. Our answer: with a dinner party! We decided to call it The Fifty Third Dinner and we would let the guests do the cooking. We would invite everyone who had attended one of our dinners during the year and ask them to bring a dish. As we had hosted well over a hundred guests, however, we were stumped as to how to fit everyone in our tiny house. Michael's solution was to hold an all-day affair. From ten in the morning until ten at night, our door would be open. The only problem was that the fifty-third

Sunday fell on January 2. I was concerned that a lot of people would still be nursing hangovers and after all the holiday revelry, just plain tired of parties.

For now we needed to shelf that problem: a more pressing concern about guests was developing. All seats for the final two Sundays in November had been filled for weeks, but I was starting to get a number of calls from friends who had to beg off because of illness and unexpected visits by family members. By the third week of November, I found myself with no guests at all on the books. Even with my new-found resolve, would I fail to complete my challenge? I couldn't allow that to happen. When a flurry of phone calls did not produce anyone for our Sunday dinner, I started to panic. After preparing forty-six dinner parties, I was in danger not of being defeated by fatigue or pain, but by over-booked and flu-stricken friends. That was not going to happen even if it meant I'd have to cruise the streets of Sonoma looking for people to drag to my house. Thankfully, I wasn't reduced to that.

My friend Karen agreed to adjust her holiday party schedule and my brother Bill returned early from a visit with my son in Shelter Cove. It may not have been a full table, but at least I could call it a dinner party. My unbroken record of Sunday dinners would remain intact.

In early December, it was clear that as long as I did not suffer a serious attack and at least some people showed up every week, I'd actually finish the challenge. By now, word had spread far and wide, too. I was getting phone calls from newspaper reporters and e-mails from around the country. Suddenly everyone wanted to talk with me. It was amazing. All I had done was cook dinner every Sunday; thousands of men and women did the same thing each week. But the idea that I had done this as a means of warding off MS—and that we had brought together scores of friends in the process—seemed to have struck a nerve.

Secretly, however, I was starting to feel uncomfortable with all the attention. Although the medical prognosis wasn't good going into this, at the conclusion of the year, I was still walking. I wasn't in a wheelchair. How could I be viewed as an inspiration? I was reveling in a sense of personal accomplishment over finishing this challenge, but at the same time, I was feeling a little embarrassed at the admiration this was generating.

I began to believe that if this whole thing didn't end tragically it hadn't been a legitimate challenge after all. It took my friend Sue to straighten me out.

"I need to talk, Sue," I sobbed into the phone.

Every woman needs a friend who doesn't ask why, but just acts. "I'll be right there" was her immediate response.

"I spent the afternoon crying on a bench along the bike path. I was a mess."

Sue is a sensible woman. I doubt she has ever sat on a bench with mascara running down her face while joggers cut a wide berth around her, but she displayed not the slightest hint of disapproval.

"Why?"

"Everyone thought I was going to end up in a wheelchair and it didn't happen. Now there are all these newspaper stories coming out and people are asking me to speak at their Rotary meetings. What the hell am I going to say? I cooked dinner every Sunday? Why should anyone admire me for that? I'm going to make a fool of myself."

"So, let me get this straight. You think people will be disappointed because you didn't become completely disabled? That no one will be interested in your story because it didn't end badly?"

"Well, yes. I guess that's it, although it sounds pretty ridiculous when you put it that way."

"Because it is. You came up with the novel idea to cook your way through your problems and you succeeded. Your drive and your attitude is what everyone admires. There are plenty of sad stories in the world. People love hearing about someone who actually triumphs over their adversity."

"But that's the problem. I didn't get sick enough for this to be a triumph."

"You will never know why you did not get as sick as the doctors thought you would. Why couldn't it have been the fact that you placed a goal in front of yourself every week and never backed down from the challenge? That your unique approach to battling MS has something to do with why you are still walking?"

"Maybe it was just all that wine I drank. I drowned my immune system in pinot noir."

"That could've been it. And we all got to enjoy the cure with you. That's where the story is, Ronda. You didn't ask your friends to just sit back and watch you suffer. You invited us to enjoy life with you for as long as possible. Your guests, the people who read about your story, all who shared in this adventure have benefited."

"You think what we did was helpful in some way?"

"I know it was. You remember when I told you that my family had drifted apart after my father died?"

"Yes, of course."

"I got to thinking about it and called everyone, my brother, my sisters and my mother. I told them I had a friend who even though she was fighting a serious illness managed to bring together her friends and family members every single Sunday for almost an entire year now. I told them we ought to be able to pull off a potluck with our family at least once a month."

"Are you kidding me?"

"We've had two dinners together so far. I was waiting for a chance to tell you about it. It is really wonderful, Ronda. It is bringing my family back together. I would not have made that phone call if it weren't for you."

She had me in tears again.

# Menu:

## Homemade ricotta
with warm bread
Classic Caesar salad

## Rabbit ragu
over creamy polenta

## Olive oil cake
with pistachio gelato

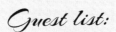

# Guest list:

Fred & Stevie
Bill & Rose
Barb
Meg, a reporter from
the local newspaper

I was thrilled that Stevie and her husband were making the two hour drive from Auburn, California, to attend one of our gatherings. Stevie was not only my friend, she was also the daughter of one of the dearest people I've ever known. Stevie's mother Fran and I met through a program called "Friendly Visitors." I had volunteered with the organization, agreeing to spend an hour a week providing companionship to an elderly shut-in. My intention was to do something nice for someone else, but in the end, I got far more than I gave. Fran became my champion, my confidant and my beloved friend. She also gave me one of the most precious gifts one human being can give to another; she asked me to be at her side as she neared death. In doing so, she showed me how peaceful and gently one can leave this life. Her last conversation in this world was with me. Her last words were "I love you." She will live on in my heart forever.

Bill and Rose also drove miles to come to our gathering. They are a modern day version of George Burns and Gracie Allen. With their constant good-natured snipes at each other, they gave the evening a wonderful light-hearted tone and kept all of us laughing. This was one night I really needed their witty repartee.

With a newspaper reporter at the table I was feeling the pressure. I chose to stick with stand-bys, making my rabbit ragu for the main course, the ricotta and the olive oil cake. After fifty weeks I certainly had these recipes down pat. This was definitely not a time to be experimental, start sipping the cooking sherry, or wait until the last minute to get things rolling.

I had to get past my nervousness over all the exposure and endure having my photo taken after nearly a year of fattening dinners. But the excitement of my looming success had me giddy with anticipation. Meg took me aside to ask me her questions.

I told her about the nearly one hundred and thirty people we were able to gather together in our home. Our guest list had included friends ranging in age from five to eighty-five. Some were die-hard Republicans, some staunch liberals. We enjoyed the giggles of children and the wisdom of our elders. What they all shared in common was the willingness to laugh with us, cry with us and tell us their stories.

The year taught us that the effort we put forth, the investment we made in friendships was perhaps one of the most worthwhile we had ever made. Through our year of dinner parties, we had learned that simply labeling someone as a friend was not at all the same thing as actually being a friend.

But some friendships are not meant to last forever. I had issued fifty-two invitations to Kathy and she had declined every one. When a person says no to you fifty-two times in a row, they are sending you a powerful message. It was time to say goodbye. They say everyone comes into your life for a reason, a season or a lifetime. I had been certain Kathy was a lifer. I was wrong. Apparently she was destined to be with me only for a portion of my life. She had been there to help me over the rough patches, cheer me through my victories and listen patiently to every new scheme. She was the epitome of a best friend. I would miss her deeply. But with all of the new people we had met over the year I now had an army of friends. I could look back at all of the years Kathy and I spent together and simply smile at the wonderful memories.

There's an old German saying, "That which doesn't kill you, makes you stronger." This year had not just made me strong. It helped me to believe in myself again. Each week I was able to cross off the calendar was another step away from the ledge. Every time I refused to give into fatigue and pain was another salvo fired at MS.

A friend told me, "You surprised us all. I would have never guessed you were this resilient." It was not unexpected that my friends and family were taken aback by my newfound capacity for perseverance. I had allowed much less significant adversities to send me into emotional tailspins.

How had this, surely the most serious threat I had ever faced, been the one I was able to overcome? Where, within my wimpy, whiny self had I found courage? There isn't one answer to that question.

There was a time when Michael and I believed we had life figured out. We had our retirement secured, money in the bank and a plan for the future that included a host of adventures. I had gone back to school to finish my degree in philosophy and I was excited about the new opportunities I saw stretching before me. Our four sons had been successfully launched in life. Our future seemed protected from nearly every possible peril. Most of all, we had formed a bond between us few couples ever manage to achieve: a marriage rich in laughter and love. Life was good, too good to allow Multiple Sclerosis to destroy it.

Michael had already lost one woman he loved to MS. It was an unimaginably cruel twist of fate that thirty-five years after his mother's death, he was in danger of losing another. If it took every bit of tenacity I could muster, every ounce of courage I could dredge up, I had to protect him from that fate. If a good attitude was going to help, I'd cop the best anyone had ever seen.

Michael could write the primer for how to handle a sick spouse. It must be nearly impossible to strike the right balance between showing concern and being overly protective. His calm, supportive voice saw me through many a crisis, but he never hovered over me or lost his confidence in my ability to persevere. He stood patiently by as I labored up each step, only offering a hand when requested. His confidence in me fostered the self-assurance I needed to face the challenge. I couldn't possibly let him down.

But perhaps most of all, the impetus for completing this journey came from those who traveled with me. The multitude of friends we amassed along the way taught me some of the most important lessons in life. Their willingness to share their stories, to offer the gift of their friendship was a compelling reason to keep going. The support and camaraderie they provided infused me with a resolve I never knew I could access. It felt as though I had my own private cheering section, but in truth, we were all cheering for each other in one way or another.

Everyone needs to be heard, to be understood. At our dinners, you had the undivided attention of at least seven other people. If you needed a good laugh, an evening away from the issues of your life, all you had to do was show up at the front door. Whether you hungered for relief from loneliness or just for a nice slice of pizza, we had what you needed. Sue was right. There was plenty of healing to go around, and it was inspiring to know that we had brought about all of this through our gatherings. It was all the motivation I needed.

As our final gathering neared we began to consider with whom we should share it. There were so many who had traveled this road with us and who were instrumental in making it successful. Sue and Alan were our most frequent and favorite guests, so they were a natural first choice, but they were not available that evening.

Scott, as well, had attended many dinners and was really a member of the family now. We couldn't imagine a final dinner without his company. Fortunately he was able to join us and planned on bringing along his date, a woman he had known in high school. Best of all, Michael's youngest son, Tony, who had not been able to join us before because of work constraints was making the long drive up from San Luis Obispo to take part.

Molly and I have enjoyed a friendship that spans decades. We've talked our way through countless dilemmas over a cup of coffee and we've comforted one another through difficult health issues. I was thrilled when I learned that she and Steve could adjust their schedule to be at this final dinner. They were a perfect addition to this special guest list.

My old high school buddy, Gary, also called to say that he could join us. Now I would have someone from nearly every chapter of my life at the table.

# December 26th – Gathering number fifty-two

## Menu:

### Homemade ricotta
with freshly baked bread

### Field greens
with mandarin
orange vinaigrette

### Braised short ribs
over rosemary fettuccini

### Olive oil cake
with vanilla gelato

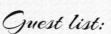

### Guest list:

Molly & Steve
Gary
Scott and Julie
Tony

For our final gathering I chose the meal with which I began the year, those magnificent braised short ribs. I looked around our gathering table and realized this just might be one of the best nights of my life.

I had reached my goal. I had managed to ward off the worst that MS had thrown at me and in the process we had solidified friendships, brought together family members and developed new alliances that were certain to last for years to come. If indeed 2010 turns out to be my last year to do all that I enjoy in life, so be it. After all, how many people are living the last good year of their life and don't know it? I had the opportunity to make mine incredible, to fill it with as much joy and laughter as possible, to gather together friends and family and to lovingly cook for them. In every way imaginable the year had been a triumph, a victory over obstacles that once seemed insurmountable.

And the view from the top of the mountain was awesome.

A week later we opened our door to guests one more time. Our fifty-third gathering was attended by more than sixty friends, with people streaming in all day carrying platters of food and bottles of wine. Every chair, every cushion and nearly all the floor space was taken up by guests with full plates balanced on their laps. Many had not met before and were eager to exchange stories about the gatherings they had attended, recalling the tales they had heard and the meals they had loved. There was lots of laughter over failed recipes, the smoke alarm (they had heard it!) and some of Michael's humorous questions.

Throughout the day friends let us know what the dinners had meant to them. A woman who had lost her husband told me how she would sometimes go for days without speaking to another person. The loneliness was crushing. Then she met Michael and me and got on our guest list. From that day forward she knew that a room full of lively conversation and the companionship of a table of new friends was only an e-mail away.

After everyone left, I found a small book that Sue had brought and placed on a table for friends to leave messages about their experiences with us over the year. Their words filled me with the realization that what we had done, the effort we had put forth, was meaningful in ways I had not even considered.

One young couple wrote, "We learned that great friends come in all ages and to never underestimate the power of the human will to entertain, even if faced with medical adversity. We also learned that Michael is great to wine taste with and Neil Diamond is alive and well, in vinyl no less! I also met a dog I actually like (thanks Bella!)."

Bella was actually mentioned several times. Another guest wrote, "We can't forget what Bella brought to the whole experience. She gave us all a lesson on the power of focused attention. Is there anyone who doesn't just absolutely adore her?"

Another told us, "Even though you made it look easy, I'm so aware of how much work you did to make the food amazing. But, we also sensed that it was much more than just a meal with friends. We really enjoyed hearing from people with differing points of view. Whether it was politics, religion, sports or travel, we got the feeling everyone's opinion was respected."

And we were surprised to discover that others were actually considering taking the baton from us and running with it.

One woman told us, "I truly feel the motivation to make 'a gathering table' effort myself this coming year. Thank you for opening your heart and soul ... and kitchen ... to make the world a better place." Another said, "You reinforced for us how special it is to sit down with friends around dinner. We're going to start planning a party for next weekend!"

It was the best consequence we could imagine from our dinners. If we were truly able to inspire our friends to keep this all going then we would have really accomplished something wonderful.

Finally there was the simple notation, "So Ronda, many thanks again for taking us on this adventure with you and Michael."

It had been an adventure, a marvelous journey we could not have made alone. It took scores of people willing to come to our table, sharing their stories and the gift of their friendship.

Focusing on the curse of Multiple Sclerosis was a choice I could have made. I could have just accepted the limitations of the disease and restricted myself to a life of frailty. But I would have missed so much. All the friends, all the laughter, all the great food and wine. By choosing to revel in the blessing instead, I was able to discover how much I actually appreciated the "blurse" life had handed me.

# *Epilogue*

It is early in the morning on a foggy day on Avila Beach. Michael has left to attend to the business of his Central Coast wine magazine. Bella and I are sitting together listening to the waves slamming against cliffs that are just steps from a small patio off the back of our hotel room. It is to here, room 518, that Michael and I fled having been told that I would die a blind quadriplegic. Three years to the day have passed since that dreadful night. I scratch Bella's ears and she leans into me. That small movement pulls me back into this moment and away from thoughts of how close I came to missing out on one of the best years of my life. I can now let go of the memory of how compelling those cliffs were when I was faced with what I thought would be an unbearably wretched existence. Back then I could not have imagined how much joy awaited me. Three years and I am still walking. I am still the victor in my battle against Multiple Sclerosis.

I love the beach even when the air is thick with a damp, briny mist, when the waves are barely discernible through the white blanket of fog that hugs the coastline. Sunshine is overrated here. With colors too bright to be ignored and everything in sharp focus, there's little room for introspection. This day is perfect. I've come back to this spot to reflect on my journey and I need a soft, gray canvas for my memories.

I'll never know if the doctors were wrong. Perhaps I could have simply planted myself on the couch, wallowing in self-pity, and still arrived here today without a wheelchair. Maybe those pesky immune cells never planned to take out the vital areas of my spinal column or invade the regions of my brain and optic nerves in the first place. It is conceivable all the time I spent in my kitchen trying to ward off this disease was entirely unnecessary.

Everyone who faces a challenging illness or event in life discovers how fervently a good attitude is endorsed. I couldn't stomach my story being touted as yet another example of how merely thinking positively can change the course of your life, though. Anyone who has spent time on a hospital gurney looking up at grim faces knows there are some hurdles you cannot clear just by employing a perky disposition. The last thing I want to do is add to anyone's burden by suggesting otherwise. My tale is not about bucking up.

Simply put, it is a story about the power of love and pasta...and what happened when two people asked scores of others to share both with them.

Michael, Bella and I are still enjoying life in Sonoma, still taking long walks on the beach together, and still dreaming of a world free of Multiple Sclerosis.

To follow our on-going saga, please visit my website at www.thegatheringtable.net and sign up for my monthly newsletter.

Made in the USA
Charleston, SC
02 January 2014